BEST CANADIAN ESSAYS 2024

Edited by Marcello Di Cintio

Biblioasis
Windsor, Ontario

FIRST EDITION
ISBN 978-1-77196-564-4 (Trade Paper)
ISBN 978-1-77196-565-1 (eBook)

Guest edited by Marcello Di Cintio
Copyedited by Rachel Ironstone
Series designed by Ingrid Paulson
Typeset by Vanessa Stauffer

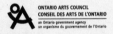

Canada Council
for the Arts

Conseil des Arts
du Canada

ONTARIO ARTS COUNCIL
CONSEIL DES ARTS DE L'ONTARIO
an Ontario government agency
un organisme du gouvernement de l'Ontario

Canada

ONTARIO | ONTARIO
CREATES | CRÉATIF

Published with the generous assistance of the Canada Council for the Arts, which last year invested $153 million to bring the arts to Canadians throughout the country, and the financial support of the Government of Canada. Biblioasis also acknowledges the support of the Ontario Arts Council (OAC), an agency of the Government of Ontario, which last year funded 1,709 individual artists and 1,078 organizations in 204 communities across Ontario, for a total of $52.1 million, and the contribution of the Government of Ontario through the Ontario Book Publishing Tax Credit and Ontario Creates.

PRINTED AND BOUND IN CANADA

CONTENTS

Marcello Di Cintio

INTRODUCTION

When my friends at Biblioasis asked me to compile this volume of Canada's finest essays of 2022, I felt honoured and flattered. At least at first. Having now completed this task, I confess that I found this assignment profoundly difficult. Not only because I haven't found a definition of "essay" that satisfies me. And not just because selecting only fourteen essays from my stacks of journals and magazines was difficult, which is something every editor of this series has intoned before me.

The main reason for my troubles was the time we live in. Or, perhaps more accurately, the time we've lived through. Two years of virus-borne anxiety had reduced my ability to consume art, literary and otherwise, to bingeing mediocre television and scrolling through Twitter rants. My attention span had shortened to the point that the cartons of magazines and literary journals that arrived at my door intimidated me. I felt paralyzed. I should've felt grateful. How could I give these essays—and, especially, the writers who composed them—the attention they deserved when my attention was so hobbled?

The answer, it turned out, was the essays themselves. Within those fearsome boxes were essays that did more than simply entertain, educate, and enlighten. Their excellence broke through my personal doldrums. These fourteen essays compelled me to think deeply about things, such as prisons, peacocks, and jars of garlic, I hadn't thought of before. But their real achievement was inspiring me to think deeply at all.

We live in a profoundly, dangerously, incurious time. We feel we know all that we need to know, believe what we're comfortable believing, and reject that which makes us feel good rejecting. But each essay in this collection shifted my mind's gears through humour or pathos or through the simple beauty of the prose. Each surprised me in some way.

The best essays bring you in to a world you know nothing about and, occasionally, into worlds you feel grateful for having never known. Kate Gies's "Foreign Bodies" brings the reader into the Hospital for Sick Children's reconstructive surgery ward: a microworld of kids who, Gies writes, are "under construction. Cut to fit the shapes of other kids, but never quite fitting." Gies seems uninterested in our pity or repulsion. She wants to show the tiny community these children have created—with *Frogger* and stolen Popsicles and half-hour cartoons, reminding us that the whimsy and rebellion of childhood blooms even in trauma's fallow soil.

Near the end of Sandy Pool's "I Love Lucy," the author explains that her "essay is not about my fake mother Lucille Ball or my fake mother Lucy Ricardo. This essay is about slapstick, and the sight gags we use to mediate the pain of not being able to be ourselves." There is no shortage of essays about mothers, but I've never read an essay that imagines the grandmother-mother-daughter relationship through the prism of classic television.

It's easy to see why Pool adopts this lens. The complications of sitcom life quickly and easily resolve. Though our mouths be stuffed with chocolate, we know the conveyor belt will stop before the commercial break. But our real-life mothers' real-life failings don't follow such scripts. They're as messy as a blouse full of broken eggs, and less funny. But at least love remains when the credits finally roll.

There is a kind of slapstick motherhood in Nicole Boyce's "One Route, Over and Over" too. In the essay, Boyce describes the nighttime drives she and her husband must take to lull their infant son to sleep. The nocturnal neighbourhood tours, fast food anniversary dinners, and references to Sandra Bullock speeding bus movies are ridiculous in the way that parenthood often is.

Parents know the tiny worlds our tiniest babies create for us. Boyce's entire universe consists of two frazzled parents and their infant son, confined to the cramped interior of a seven-year-old Jetta. Children shrink our lives and deprive us of sleep while also granting us purpose. "I'd drive all night if I had to," Boyce writes. We all would.

There is no such lightness in Hamed Esmaeilion's "The Fight of My Life." The account of an Iranian couple who meet under the watchful eye of their government, fall in love in spite of it all, fear reprisals, and move to Canada where they will be free sounds like something we've heard before. But everything turns on the unpredictable tragedy that upends this story, namely the downing of Ukraine International Airlines Flight 752 in January 2020, which killed 176 people, including the author's wife, Parisa, and their daughter, Reera. The essay is both a crushing memoir of loss and regret and an angry political screed against the system responsible.

It is also crushingly beautiful. Early in the essay, the author writes of his love for Parisa, his quitting smoking because he knew she didn't approve. In the dark wake of her death, he writes: "I've cut my hair short and grown a beard; Parisa did not like it this way. But no one who is alive cares what my hair looks like. I smoke now." That last sentence, three short words, devastated me more than anything else I read this year.

While Esmaeilion lost his wife and daughter to the kind of disaster that made world news, Robert Colman lost his father to a more intimate tragedy. I read many essays about caring for an aging parent—the topic could be its own subgenre—but I read few as quietly beautiful as Colman's "Every Saturday."

Like "The Fight of My Life," this essay didn't teach me anything surprising. I think we all know what can befall our loved ones, and ourselves, as the years pile on. It was Colman's craft that struck me. "Every Saturday" is an essay about poetry that reads like a poem. An essay about the daily repetitions of a gentle man that is, itself, a series of gentle repetitions. Perhaps even more so, the essay answered the question of how writers mine art from intimate and ordinary tragedies.

David Huebert offers a similar artistic rendering of an otherwise ordinary event in "Flesh Made Burn: A Vasectomy Revenant." The essay hits all the nerdy buttons for me. An anatomy lesson for those who didn't pay enough attention in high school biology class. A bit of medical etymology. References to Dante, Hemingway, and, oddly, the musical *Cats*. But while the incident motivating the essay is coldly clinical, in Huebert's hands it becomes a moving meditation on male fragility and fatherhood in ways I didn't expect from a "dick and balls" essay:

What I have realized in four short years as a parent, is that children breed love. Making children reveals that love is exponential—the more you make, the more love fills your world. To make tiny humans, then, is to populate the world with love.

"Do No Harm," Sadiqa de Meijer's essay about studying and practising medicine in a prison town, engendered sympathy for the voiceless populations behind bars. De Meijer reveals how in the desire to punish and rehabilitate, we on the outside are discouraged from feeling anything other than fear for the men behind the walls and barbed wire. De Meijer brings us into the hospital rooms where prisoners are also patients. These men are incarcerated not just by the bars on the cells, but by the cuffs binding their wrists and ankles to hospital beds, and then by the anaesthesia rendering them triply imprisoned.

De Meijer doesn't excuse anyone's behaviour but cautions against simply focusing on the short story of what they've done. Each prisoner harbours a more fulsome tale of all that's been done to them. Long narratives—sometimes generations long—have led these men inside. De Meijer acknowledges that these men, for all their misdeeds, are loved, especially by their children. "I could almost see their love and longing and anger for their fathers," de Meijer writes, "tethered and drifting from the razor-wired walls like threads of spider silk."

"Ruffled Feathers: How Feral Peacocks Divided a Small Town" provides a quirky palate cleanser for all this seriousness. Lyndsie Bourgon's essay about the feral peacocks of Naramata is a delight, and not just for cruelly funny revelations like "other than from an aesthetic perspective, peafowl are essentially useless." Haven't we all felt this way about ourselves at one time or another?

Bourgon's essay does what all great essays do: finds the big story in the small one, the meaning in the minuscule. The essay ponders what happens when a community known for one thing, and proudly so, begins to grow weary of it. "For Naramata," Bourgon writes, "its peafowl became a fulcrum of what the town is and what it wants to be." All communities must come to terms with such questions of identity sooner or later. Perhaps all people must too. If only we all had Bourgon to chronicle our ruffled feathers.

Acadia Currah's short essay with a long title, "Femme Fatales and the Lavender Menace," offers an intimate portrait of the author's adolescent heart. In this piece, we meet the writer as a teenage girl trying to account for her crushes on other teenage girls. While full of delicious details about "Lip Smacker" kisses, "high-ponytails," and a stale Dorito that "hits your tongue like communion bread," this is no saccharine "how I learned I'm gay" narrative. Like all the essays in this collection, Currah dives deep. As she discovers who she is—someone who loves like a girl, holding "people warm inside [her] body"—she also learns who the boys really are, namely creatures with "shark teeth" whose hungry looks make her stomach turn.

The short sentence that closes the essay, "And you like girls," distills all the fretting, confusion, and learning into four-word simplicity. And, like Esmaeilion's "I smoke now," it's perfect.

As an Italian-Canadian, cuisine-based pomposity is as much my cultural birthright as the *o* at the end of my name. I admit I'm one of the snobs accused in Gabrielle Drolet's "In Defense of Garlic in a Jar: How Food Snobs Almost Ruined My Love of Cooking." Or at least I was until I read her essay. Drolet revealed the ableism in my comfortable snobbery, an arrogance I'd always considered harmless.

There is a lesson here that expands outside the kitchen. The age we dwell in regards public insult and dismissal as a virtue. We identify ourselves, as loudly as possible, by what we reject. (Another shameful societal quirk the pandemic turbo-charged.) Drolet reminded me we're far better off defining ourselves by what we love. And, thanks to her, I now buy pre-peeled garlic.

Daniel Allen Cox's deliciously titled "You Can't Blame Movers for Everything Broken" unsettled me. I didn't need to know that the strangers we hire to move our stuff know far more about our lives than we could imagine. There are lines in here I'll remember the next time I'm packing up my bookshelves and my underwear drawer.

Cox's chief achievement in this essay, though, is to render an activity as commonplace as moving house into something fascinating. This isn't a cheap celebration of the "box donkeys" whose labour usually goes unsung. Instead, Cox has penned a meditation on an occupation far more nuanced and psychological than it seems on the surface—and gilded this dusty job with beautiful prose.

Fiona Tinwei Lam takes on the pandemic in "Bad Days." She begins with another emotion I've felt over these last few years: a "long submerged sense of unease." For Lam, though, this stems not just from the pandemic itself but from the anti-Asian racism that flared in its wake. "The present equation is simple," Lam writes, "all Asians are Chinese; all Chinese embody the virus; you are the virus."

And Lam brought receipts. While highly personal, "Bad Days" is also deeply researched, enriched by history and statistics.

What results is more than just an account of what it meant to be Asian during a crisis many blamed on Asians, but what it has always meant to be Asian in Canada. "Bad Days" strikes against Canada's maple-dipped self-image, inspires both empathy and rage, and warns that "no matter how you prepare, it seems more 'bad days' are surely to come."

Jenny Hwang also uses her Asian heritage as the engine for her essay, but while Lam projects her personal experience of the pandemic outward to speak about the Asian-Canadian community, Hwang's "Silkworms" peers inward. Her grandmother's translated writings connect her to a matriarch she never knew. Hwang discovers where she'd inherited her own sense of sadness and justice. For Hwang, reading her grandmother's treatise on silkworms is akin to reading her own secret origin story.

Like "Bad Days," "Silkworms" is a pandemic essay: a tale of a burned-out mom dealing first with isolation, then with the anxiety borne of the world reopening. These are feelings nearly every parent coped with over the last few years. We all struggled to find joy and hope somewhere. Inspired by her grandmother, Hwang found hers in the quiet life cycle of caterpillars, and the "lifting and landing" of butterflies. I felt envious of this.

Just as Hwang found post-pandemic comfort in the dance of butterflies, Kyo Maclear's mother found post-divorce solace in art. In "Giverny," Maclear writes of her mother's divorce: "A marriage is a counterweight, and while she had never been compliantly or happily married, it was frightening to her, unimaginable, to suddenly spring forth into the world."

Maclear allows us to stand beside her mother, in the rain, on the edge of Claude Monet's lagoon. As her mother's known world collapses, she seeks out the unwavering pleasure found in

Monet's most famous paintings. Haven't we all felt this way in the last few years? In the midst of so much upheaval and uncertainty, we're all Maclear's mother, yearning for something beautiful to rely on.

At the end of Kyo Maclear's essay, I found the line that describes all the authors in this collection, the line that will end my essay about these great essayists. "I would like to be a writer who, if I cannot convey things in themselves, captures the air as it touches the world." Isn't this what all great essayists do? Shouldn't this be every writer's goal?

Lyndsie Bourgon

———

RUFFLED FEATHERS

How Feral Peacocks Divided a Small Town

It began with a peahen named Pearl. She was the only female in a trio of peafowl that once freely roamed the small town of Naramata, British Columbia. Her chicks had the bright-blue bodies and metallic-green tail feathers that make the male members of her species iconic, but Pearl's colouring was rare: her entire body and tail feathers were a shimmering white.

Peafowl in Naramata have been traced back to at least 2010, though some say Pearl arrived in the early 2000s, rumoured to have escaped from a nearby ranch. Over the years, Pearl mated with one of her chicks, and the flock eventually expanded as she continued to breed. Still, when and how the birds first arrived in town is a mystery. In a book of Naramata history, community historian Craig Henderson concedes that, really, "no one knows."

Perhaps, though, no one wants the blame. The peafowl eventually became a source of tension in this quaint community on Okanagan Lake, in southern BC's wine country. As their numbers grew, they made more and more of the town's infrastructure and environment their own. Tourists loved them, and for some residents, they were a welcome addition to the town's ambiance. Some people provided bird food throughout the winter or built shelters in their yards and filled them with hay or blankets, "kind of like the manger," recalls local singer Yanti Sharples.

The peafowl seemed to follow a sort of daily migration, commuting from yard to yard, says local librarian Joanne Smiley. But the birds also ate from those yards, helping themselves to vegetable patches and petunia plants. The peafowl were, after all, wild, and they roamed and made roosts wherever they pleased. They peered into windows, staring at their own reflections. They climbed on top of cars so often, leaving deep scratches from their long talons, that people started putting large stuffed animals on the hoods of their cars, says Sharples, like fluffy scarecrows. One peafowl was known to sleep in the branches of a ponderosa pine outside the public library and peck at the flowerpots out front.

What small towns become known for is sometimes a product of chance and often not universally welcomed. For Naramata, its peafowl became a fulcrum of what the town is and what it wants to be. Every Thursday, the peafowl could be seen chasing the garbage truck. Their droppings littered the streets, and their shrill cries echoed throughout the quiet town. To Smiley, it sometimes sounded like a silly cackle. "You might think, *They look beautiful, so they might sound beautiful.* They do not."

*

Other than from an aesthetic perspective, peafowl are essentially useless. Though, if English poet John Ruskin is to be believed, the "most beautiful things in the world are the most useless; peacocks and lilies, for instance." Mostly, they just walk around and put on a show. For such a big bird, they have a negligible impact on the balance of an urban ecosystem—apart from a nibble here or a peck there. Likewise, not much pushes back: in North American cities, predators of peafowl are most likely to be dogs or raccoons. Beauty is the peafowl's saving grace. Their feathers are long, colourful beacons splayed confidently, and the plumage is a protector of the species: peahens are attracted to peacocks with long tail feathers and piercing ocelli, the round, eye-shaped tips of the feather. It so happens that the same aesthetic trait attracts gawking humans too.

Even when his tail is not on display, a peacock's feathers are clumped in a long train that flows behind him as he walks, a veil-like accessory. "If they weren't beautiful, no one would love them," says Smiley. "And they are exceptionally beautiful." That they became emblematic of Naramata speaks in many ways to the people who live there rather than to the animals themselves.

Situated on some of the most coveted land in the Okanagan region, Naramata has historically enticed creative, one might say *eccentric*, residents. While the rest of the Okanagan wine region has cultivated a polished, Instagram-filtered glow, Naramata has held fast to the bygone off-the-grid pace that drew small homesteaders and orchard operators to the region in the 1960s and '70s. The peafowl came to fit the image of the town, which has been described as "bench bohemian" (a reference to the Naramata Bench, a subzone of the Okanagan Valley), "artistically unconventional," and, once, "a will-work-for-crystals economy." As tourism boomed in the region and orchards were tilled into vineyards, Naramata's peafowl became an attraction in their own right.

Witnessing such eye-catching fowl idling around urban areas is not unique to Naramata, but peafowl differ from other birds that are symbolic but also native, like the eagles that soar above Vancouver, the seagulls that flit around Halifax, or even the Canada geese that strut on golf courses across the country. All these birds bring annoyance to human communities in much the same way peafowl do—noise, droppings, property damage, territorial aggression—but those inconveniences might be easier to brush off because they're local. They're *ours*, part of the natural world we have built our lives in.

Peafowl, though, native to the Indian subcontinent and Southeast Asia, are an introduced species in North America. They were brought to populate hobby farms or the estates of (often wealthy) landowners who wanted to see a peacock silently glide and unfurl its feathers in an elegant display. But the birds have often been left behind when those owners moved, or they have escaped from properties that aren't secure. In places like Naramata, they have then become feral.

Peafowl are not covered by BC's Wildlife Act or any other provincial or territorial wildlife act, which makes it difficult to responsibly remove them from a municipality where they roam free. They're also not considered game birds. And to tamper with their eggs is an offense punishable by a $300 fine. In 2019, dozens of feral peafowl dominated the Sullivan Heights neighbourhood of Surrey, BC, leading to complaints by residents at their wits' end. It was a small farm that had brought the peacocks to Surrey in the first place: when the farmland was developed, the birds stuck to their territory.

The municipality struck up a pilot project, trapping and putting the birds up for adoption through the Surrey Animal

Resource Centre and relocating them to wildlife sanctuaries, zoos, and farms. The eventual trapping program was rolled out slowly, though, and over a year later, a dozen still remained in Sullivan Heights. Some residents told the media that they wanted the peafowl to stay; one resident, reportedly frustrated by the city's inaction, felled a large tree in his yard that had become a popular roosting spot. The peafowl in both Naramata and Surrey came to exist in a grey zone—neither wildlife nor pets, beloved and despised, and impossible to legislate.

*

In September 2010, a community meeting about Naramata's peafowl population was held at the OAP (Old-Age Pensioners) Hall. The meeting, which filled the hall to capacity, was sparked by an anonymous homeowner who, worried about expanding brood size, had hired a trapper from nearby Peachland to capture Pearl and her chicks and move them to a petting zoo. The trapper, Larry Fehr, had built a large wooden trap on the homeowner's property. "This was the first time I ever caught a peacock," he says in Henderson's book on Naramata's history.

Fehr captured the birds on private property, but their status—somewhere between wild and domesticated—meant that they didn't technically belong to anyone. This, naturally, ruffled feathers. The line had long been blurred between wild animals surviving in an urban environment and beloved pets who belonged to the town. In the days that followed, it emerged that three of Pearl's chicks had died after being transported to the zoo. A delegation of townspeople visited the zoo to check on its conditions.

By the September meeting, tensions were high. The town was divided over what to do about Pearl, now some sixty kilometres away; over how her relocation had taken place; and over the fact that a trapper had been called without a town meeting. "I love Pearl dearly," said resident Carol Shea, according to local news site *MyNaramata*. "I've admired her fabulous mothering instincts with her chicks. I really love our Naramata peafowl…But I don't want twenty or thirty of them."

Another attendee suggested forming a bird society to bring Pearl home and provide public education around peafowl care. No one agreed to join, and as Henderson writes in his book, the proposal was shut down by a regional district employee who cautioned that anyone who brought back Pearl and her chicks would need to enclose them to prevent them from roaming the town unchecked. Essentially, someone would need to take ownership of the birds, turning them into pets. Resident Carol Allen later commented on *MyNaramata* that this sentiment "hung over the meeting like the ghost at a banquet, intimidating attendees into a state of paralysis."

The meeting, it was agreed, was essentially useless. Pearl (who had been renamed Naramata at her new home) remained a resident of the petting zoo. According to *MyNaramata*, though, "most attendees learned something about peafowl, and just about everyone felt that the chance to talk about an issue with neighbours is always an exercise in community building."

"After the meeting," an attendee later commented on the local news site, "I wondered how long Naramata will remain distinctive…"

*

The trapper left behind three peacocks to roam free in Naramata. When one was killed by a dog, someone commented on

MyNaramata that it was as if one of her children had been killed. The two remaining birds were dubbed Peter and Kevin. They lived in the ponderosa pines near the public library and moved freely around town for more than a decade.

Three more peafowl reportedly appeared on Naramata's streets in 2014, four years after Pearl and her chicks had been relocated to the petting zoo. How they arrived in town was a mystery. "I am wondering where they came from, if it is immaculate conception, because to the best of my knowledge there is no female," said Janet McDonald, executive director of The Centre at Naramata, according to local news site *Castanet*. But the three reportedly didn't remain long.

A sort of détente was reached regarding Peter and Kevin. Knowing that they couldn't mate and expand the pack was a consolation. Some Naramata residents felt that the peacocks had essentially become an integrated part of nature in their small town. It appeared that, after so many years, Naramata had finally come to accept its resident peafowl.

In January, however, Kevin disappeared. Residents discovered iridescent blue-and-green plumage scattered in the snow at two sites: in a backyard near the library and behind the Naramata Inn. The inn posted a short eulogy on Facebook: "Kevin's swagger, regal beauty, confidence, and quirkiness will be dearly missed. Rest in power Kevin." Shortly thereafter, Peter vanished as well. It's suspected that they died by bobcat, but neither bird's carcass was ever found. Yanti Sharples wrote a memorial song for the last of the Naramata peacocks. As mysteriously as it began, the town's turbulent history with peafowl came to an end.

Naramata has recently been experiencing a culture shift—a booming housing market, glossy new vineyards, well-heeled tourism. With Kevin and Peter presumed dead, the town has lost a symbol of itself, a surprising reminder of its quirky and colourful roots.

Nicole Boyce

——————————

ONE ROUTE,
OVER AND OVER

It's mid-June, and we're driving the baby through a flash flood. When we bought this car—a seven-year-old Jetta—we did not consider its water-treading potential. We did not consider how loudly the engine might hum, or how much the car might vibrate because of its low clearance, though both these factors end up working in our favour. The Jetta gets good mileage, too, so gas station stops are few and far between.

Still, if we'd known how many hours we'd spend in our car, driving our first-born child to sleep, we would have bought something exceptional. Something as rugged and grumbly as modern safety standards would allow: a baby-oscillating machine. We would have installed a camp toilet in the back and a novelty coffee maker in the front. We would have prepared ourselves.

As it is, we drive the Jetta. More specifically, I drive the Jetta. My husband sits in the passenger seat. It wasn't raining when we left the house, but the sky was brooding and heavy; we should have known. I gun it through a puddle that's more like a mini lake. Rain streams down the windshield. Should we pull over? Maybe we should pull over. But if we pull over, the baby might wake up. And right now the baby is sleeping, cradled in his car seat like a soft little snail.

So we drive.

*

I didn't start driving until I was thirty years old. This may not seem strange to some. But in Calgary—home of oil, gas, and urban sprawl—it's unusual. Most of my friends got their licenses in their mid-teens.

I wish I could attribute my non-driving years to choice—something philosophical or pragmatic—but in truth I just failed a lot of road tests. I failed one test by popping my tires over the curb. I failed another by speeding through an uncontrolled intersection. My first test, at sixteen, was a trifecta of failure. First I botched the parallel park. Then I rolled a stop sign. Finally, as I pulled up to the driving school, I backed up too far and hit a chicken delivery car.

By the time I finally got my license, at twenty-three, I'd missed out on a sense of teenage invincibility. My heart raced when I borrowed my parents' Mazda. I held the steering wheel like a violent criminal I'd agreed to subdue until the police arrived. As I drove, my mind wailed: You are not cut out for this!!!

So I put off driving. I bought bus passes. I mooched rides. I never dreamed I'd one day drive for hours, mindlessly, as easily as breathing.

*

For weeks my husband and I eat dinner in the car. This saves us the trauma of our previous bedtime routine: bouncing the screaming baby for hours in front of the kitchen fan. In the car, the baby succumbs to sleep like gravity. My husband and I exhale, then drive for an hour before transferring the baby to his crib.

"McDonald's or Wendy's?" my husband asks. Our son rarely wakes right after passing out, so we have a window in which to pick up dinner. On a fancy night, we'll hit two drive-throughs: one for dinner and one for dessert. For our anniversary, I make my husband a card with the logos of every major fast-food chain. The caption: "Oh, the places we'll go!"

We go A LOT of places on these night drives. We go outside the city, to the Rockies, where the mountains loom over us like stately gods in profile. We explore nearby neighbourhoods, memorizing which house has the best-groomed apple tree, which house still turns on their Christmas lights. Old neighbourhoods are the best for night drives because infill developers have ripped up aging sewage pipes, leaving the streets patched and bumpy. Rock-a-bye, baby.

While we drive, we talk about the baby. We aren't sure what ails him: one doctor says colic; another says nothing serious, maybe gas ("Try cutting out dairy"). Everyone has an opinion: the baby is manipulating us; the baby is feeding off my anxiety, sucking nervous energy like a poltergeist. People mean well. But at the end of the day, when we've tried every suggestion, it's just me and my husband, bleary-eyed at 2 am, laying down our child like a live explosive.

"I just feel like . . . it's not supposed to be this difficult," my husband says one night.

Driving is our pardon. Driving is the difference between holding hands over a gear shift, sipping strawberry milkshakes, and sniping at each other because someone coughed during the bedtime bounce.

Driving is the thinnest, most necessary peace.

*

One thing that surprised me when I started driving was the sheer capacity of a car. A car is a hundred backpacks you don't have to carry. As a non-driver, potlucks required me to ride the bus with a lapful of quinoa. Now the possibilities are endless. "Yes, I brought this lemon meringue pie to share. It wasn't rained on or elbowed by someone on the train. WOULD YOU LIKE TO SEE MY EXTRA PAIR OF SHOES?"

A car is not just a means of getting somewhere: it's a home on the go. In it, you can commute without making eye contact with a single other person. And though it is convenient, a luxury, it's also isolating. Cars deprive people of accidental empathy: no conversations overheard on the #18 bus, no buskers serenading you at the train station.

In a car you are one degree removed. You are—like struggling new parents—within throwing distance of other people, but it feels like you're light years away, somewhere airless and ancient, travelling in your own glass universe.

*

We run on adrenaline. We try not to think about the safety risks of driving while sleep-deprived. About the gas bills (huge) and the fossil fuel emissions (many). We know we're lucky in many ways: not all parents have a car to drive, and the time to drive it aimlessly.

I try to atone for my carbon footprint by walking the baby in the stroller for naps. I log ten thousand, fifteen thousand steps a day. I spend a lot of time in what my husband dubs "The Bermuda Triangle": a meeting of three paths in our local park where mature trees provide shade from the heat. I eat breakfast cookies out of a Ziploc and shoot dirty looks at strangers who laugh too close to the stroller. My mental health is . . . not great.

The baby becomes more noise-sensitive, so we stop talking on our night drives. Instead, my husband strokes my neck as we travel. I become really good at planning right-hand routes so the car never comes to a long stop.

"This is basically the movie *Speed*," I whisper.

Everything feels so dire and precarious, an instant away from disaster. We are Keanu Reeves and Sandra Bullock, but our son is no villain—he's just overtired. When he's awake, I hold his warm, doughy hands and watch his sturdy legs do can-cans on our unvacuumed rug.

He is the hero of this movie.

*

My mother is a nervous driver. "You need to learn how to drive one route," she told me when I got my license. "Just one route, over and over, until you get used to the road." This sounds good in theory, but forty years after getting her license, my mom still isn't used to the road. Her greatest delight—possibly in all of life—is finding two back-to-back parking spots at the mall so she can pull straight through and avoid backing out.

And I wonder: Why do things come naturally to some people and not to others? I think of my teenage friends blasting Misfits in their Volvos. Where was their hesitancy, their stifling inexperience?

Where was their fear?

When I described my son's sleep struggles to friends and family members, and finally to a counselor, they all responded with compassion. Still, I sensed an unspoken question: Why are you going to such lengths? Why don't you just let him skip a nap? Or let him cry—it's not the end of the world.

But it's so hard, in the thick of things, to know what's reasonable and what's extreme. To find the line between compassion and excess, between instinct and common sense.

Some things come naturally, and others do not.

*

On the worst night my husband is out of town. It's August, and he's on the first business trip he's dared to take since our son was born in March. The baby throws a fit. He refuses to nap or eat. By bedtime he's so wound up that he can't fall asleep, even in the car.

Panicked, I call my mother-in-law. She races over and manages to calm my son enough that she can toss him at my exposed breast in the space between cries: a Hail Mary pass. He gloms on like one of those sticky-hands they sell in mall vending machines. Thank fucking god.

After he's nursed, I put him back in the car and he passes out. I drive and I drive and I drive. As the sun starts to set, I pause at a stop sign and reach into the back seat. I read an article about how you shouldn't let babies sleep in their car seats: there's a suffocation risk. Babies have tiny windpipes, the diameter of drinking straws. We must protect our babies' drinking straws.

So I reach back and put my hand under my son's nose. I feel the soft wonder of his breath against my fingers.

In and out.

In and out.

The sky is pink and magnificent. Summer was always my favourite season: the yawning, open-ended days that seem to roll right into each other, never bothering to truly become nights.

Tracy Chapman starts playing on the radio: "Fast Car"—a song about driving, dreaming, escape.

I smile in spite of myself. The moment feels tidal and over-whelming, awash with such uncertain beauty. It seems like forever since I've seen one: a night that feels like night.

*

I'd like to say it ended when we hired the sleep coach. When we tried the Ferber method, and then (unable to tolerate the crying anymore) the lax Ferber method, and then breastfeeding-to-sleep, and then lying down beside our son, humming lullabies.

In truth, it never fully ended.

Our son is almost two now, and for the most part he's aged out of his bedtime meltdowns. The sleep training helped a little. Time helped more. We learned that sleep is not a straight line: it's cursive.

We no longer drive at bedtime, but some nights I'm still awoken by my son's cries. I go into his dark room and sit with him in the rocking chair. I drum my legs, trying to make my body into a moving car. I picture the neighbourhoods we drove through last summer: streetlights glowing orange over community gardens. When I hear my son's breathing change, I wait five minutes before putting him back in his crib. To pass the time, I sing songs in my head—hits from the nineties I don't remember memorizing: "Building a Mystery," "5 Days in May."

It's not a perfect system. But there's a quiet confidence earned over months and months of experience. I no longer feel like I'm failing every road test. I know how to use the rear defrost.

After I lay my son down, and avoid the creaky floorboard and slink out of his room like some elegant weasel, I watch him on the video monitor. He sprawls so decadently, his hands above his head, as if sunning himself on a private beach. He is lost to his dreams. He is perfect.

And I know if I did it all over, I'd still chase it: his restful, grateful relief. That I'd go to any length, every length, trying to do my best for him.

I'd drive all night if I had to.

Robert Colman

EVERY SATURDAY

Every Saturday I visit my father, we start anew. I tell him about my travel plans while I make him lunch. I joke that Icelandic literature is essentially people drinking coffee before and after someone disappears in the snow.

The only thing to ask about his day concerns Nero, his black cat, who dependably warms his knees. This is my snow, what I tell myself. For there are few other questions he's confident answering anymore, and I'm nervous about the replies I might get, where they might lead.

"How was dinner last night? Did you go to Santo's Restaurant as usual?"

"I've been down near London this week," he replies. "Can't think why."

Nero nudges a hand to be rubbed and tended.

Of course, Dad hasn't been further from Toronto than the suburbs for some time, so I change tack. Find some classical music on the radio, a comedy show. Something he can follow minute by minute, or something that might jog a memory. Anything without coordinates in the day-to-day, where ignorance winces shame.

He picks up a book next to his chair and asks about it. A few minutes later, never having put the book down, he asks again. The cat stretches on the blanket that covers his thighs. We talk about the book, where he bought it, where he's been; I try to guide him to a topic from his past that we might expand upon. But conversation is more and more elusive, and the day slides toward a kind of failure.

*

Every Saturday I visit my father, we start anew. Last night's dinner is hazy, as is the view through the snow outside the window.

"What's for lunch today?" he says, but it's always bacon and tomato. I slice the tomatoes while Nero makes his careful way across the furniture to Dad's lap. And I wonder what to do with it, this whiteout winnowing of him, in poetry. Because that's the only place I have to contain it.

I started observing the progress of Dad's Alzheimer's on the page while we were in England five years ago, our first trip ever that was just the two of us.

Then, it was cascades of his past mingled with our tourist stops along England's left hip that came into shape on the page, trundling the borders through Shrewsbury, Ludlow, then inland to Salisbury. We spoke more of his past than we had since I was a boy. The poems were almost lists, scrawled inventories of what we were seeing, interspersed with his absences and returns.

> *Own. He names Norbury Hollow, Three*
> *Purse Lane, the rail track,*
> *the miners' placid cottages, gentles me*

"drive slow if you're not ready
for the road," which he knows—
House of Twelve Windows, blood map
of ring roads, coping the edges
of today, unbidden tomorrow.

He talked over and over about cycling to Stonehenge, drop-
ping his bike in the grass to explore. This spinning, the weight of
the chain. Five years ago, such repetition meant returning to a
tale once a day. It was almost a comfort—ironically, the repetition helped lodge his memories in my mind.

This continued, in its way, back in Canada. Each week a pub
lunch and talk about his parents, their jobs, the family scandals.
The losses. We never spoke of his disease, though, and it hid
itself most days. He could hide so much in his age, all that he was
forgetting.

A few things I'm sure he made up—stories of family members
disappearing in the wilds of the US Midwest. People I'd never
heard of. But aren't most families half-truths?

I noticed that reading frustrated him—no ability to follow
plot from day to day—but little else changed. Unless he drank,
which he did, too much. Then he'd wake in the night asking
where he was, feeling suddenly unsafe. *What is this place?* But he
wouldn't stop, just as the snow doesn't, the coffee doesn't. As my
poems don't. When I write, this repetition of stubbornness is like
waves that come back to me. The stuck click of his repetition
makes me appreciate the dirge of a villanelle or pantoum, the
weight of repeated lines hammering at the door that won't open
between writer and subject.

When I say he wandered out into the snow in his slippers
I mean there's no accounting for his movements.
He remembers nothing of panic or fear, dark houses,
ringing a doorbell to tell a neighbour he is lost.

Much like he can't account for the bruises
each time he loses his balance, each time he's mashed
like a doorbell and finds no one home,
collisions patterned into what we call a day, a week.

When I write about him waking, staring out a window, unsure of where he was, a friend comments, "Of course, poetry is all body, isn't it? Doesn't all writing have that connection?" I look back at the poems and we don't touch. It has not been erased; it simply didn't happen. I go back and describe him more, to see him better.

*

Every Saturday I visit my father, we start anew. Nero drools across his knuckles, rubbing up to him.

I'm amazed how long he hid his losses. His wife remembers him giving up the crossword, says she should have known that was a sign. I think of her birthday party two years ago, during which he sat in his chair and welcomed everyone with a laugh. I doubt he recognized a soul. He taught me this trick, the nervous laughter that welcomes in its insecurity. It's an old skill he now brings into play.

Doctors say he has an "executive mind," which means he's good at hiding his inability to remember.

"What day is it today, Dad?"

"Does it really matter? I'm retired."

Early on, I catch him out with questions I know the answers to, but this becomes more frequent. Do I do it intentionally? A kind of game? I guess part of me needs to keep track, understand where we are.

One day he tells me how he woke to see his mother standing in front of him in the room, and she said, in her laconic Cheshire accent, "What are you doing sat there?" At that point he knew she was long dead, so it shook him. I imagine other people visiting from his past to guide him safely around his house. There are times, at the beginning, when I can feel almost whimsical, writing about the fractured space he occupies, but that doesn't last.

> *When she appeared,*
> *did she seem lost?*
> *Did talc or lavender*
> *solidify the host?*

> *Was she a young mother*
> *eating bread and butter*
> *cut so thick it was corporeal?*
> *Was she hungry?*

*

Every Saturday I visit my father, we start anew. I worry that he will doubt me. For two months, my visits involve at least one discussion of where we are and who is this person who collects maps of England? And this black cat is very much like my Nero. The cat is unsteady, too, fragile, sleeping longer on his knee. I try to talk us around to other topics, his sister, the weather, the birds, but the questions repeat. He disturbs the cat, wanders from map to map on the wall in wonderment.

> *There's something in a gaze*
> *when it isn't returned,*
> *can't be given back...*

I think of our small nephew, who is at an age where he sees connections everywhere—the dimples of a knife blade, his pencil case, a picture on the wall, in each he sees eyes. As the world becomes a curious whole to him, Dad loses a synapse. I can still write a lyric in that. It still surprises without hurting. He will calm down. He will come back to me in some way yet.

*

Every Saturday I visit my father, we start anew in a space that is shrinking. Where once I would take him for lunch, I no longer feel confident that he'll be able to control his bowels, or that he won't become agitated by the voices of others in a restaurant. We have accidents, we have days I need to distract him, to calm him down.

I want so much to micromanage this situation that we eat at home. Partly to keep him safe, partly because he wakes later, most days. In the summer we sit in the yard. In the winter we move from room to room as purpose demands. Sometimes he asks when his wife will collect him. One day he wonders when his mother will arrive.

My poems shrink to pantoums and triolets, poems of repetition that return to their beginning, somehow new. Except the new is more loss.

Forty-six, watching the exits, my mouth,
but something else crouches out of sight.
The "why the fuck" of family habit.
Forty-six, watching the exits, my mouth
saying he loved me, loved me enough
for this profanity to be stifled
forty-six minutes of an hour, my mouth
an anger, resentment blotting out my sight.

Nero calls deafly from elsewhere in the house.

*

Every Saturday I visit my father, we start anew, and I worry that he might not know me. Before his condition had progressed, when he still drank, I took him to dinner. On the drive home he asked if I'd far to go. I said no, not far, not knowing that he was fishing for clues, sorting through who I might be. Only when we reached his door and he said "I'll be fine from here" did it click. So I said, "Dad, I could use a cup of tea before I go." And he said, "Good idea."

I enter with "Father" to occlude any doubts
before questions come about my name,
before this loss is confirmed.
"Father" my safe word against.

Another repetition, a ritual. The poems now are rituals, too, repetitive jostlings toward understanding. Language narrows as our lives narrow. The cat's routine is an odd comfort in this.

When I share the poem about that bewildering drive home a friend says, "You can tell there was something missing all along between these two." And she's right, of course. We have no sense of the pulse of the non-verbal connection that some families have. We are good at gathering what we can without questions and hoping for the best. Which shows how desperate he was to know why he was driving through these dark streets with some stranger from another town. How clueless I was not to catch it.

*

Every Saturday I visit my father, we start anew. This time he is still asleep at 1 pm. I am tired and dread all the questions.

> *Is there another conversation to be had? I don't know.*
> *I scrape ice from the drive instead of waking him.*
> *The shuck of blade on asphalt is its own incantation,*
> *the shudder of impact, calling of spirits. You hear?*

Once done, I go to wake him and find him staring vaguely at the ceiling. He gets up, sits at the dining room table delicately. Says, "I don't know if I'm alive or dead."

I shudder at how blank that morning must have been—knowing who you are but not where or why. Signposts didn't make sense that day, no guiding voice until I roused him. Time is flattened out. "Here" is separated out and fickle.

I joke about his age, that the jury's still out, but that he is very old indeed. He knows the tone—it is the same mocking lip of his sister. This rouses him an inch or two, and a pot of tea does much of the rest.

My poems narrow to syllables some days. They want to be close to this blankness, not to disrespect it with their will to flower. They begin to break at their conclusions, try to find their beginnings but bend and rupture. Is this poetic failure or just the necessary warp of a story?

> *Everywhere, tiered groves of olives,*
> *Romans mocking our pedestrian ambitions.*

> *So much we want to learn,*
> *though suspicion and complaint mar*

> *every path.*

*

A Saturday arrives without my father, and I begin the day believing the poems can open once again. Now the more distant past can reign. But it doesn't happen. Too soon? All the words are snapshots, small stanzas on posterboard, as if made to display at his funeral.

But they are everything I don't want at his funeral. The poems were never him. Not really. They were me, chasing him through his illness, catching what I could. And after? I am staring at photographs, but it's silence I'm sitting in. No one to answer my questions.

Daniel Allen Cox

YOU CAN'T BLAME MOVERS FOR EVERYTHING BROKEN

If you don't come from a moving family, how you become a mover is almost always accidental. Your first move is a lark, fifty bucks for a few hours of work, and before you know it, you've landed in a new job slightly askew, like a dresser put down too quickly, one that's easier to leave where it is rather than reposition.

I, on the other hand, was born with a roll of packing tape around my wrist in Montreal, the city with the second-heaviest furniture in the world. My grandfather bought a fleet of twenty-eight-foot trucks in the 1970s, so that by the time I came along bundled in bubble wrap, my fate was sealed. In the '80s, my uncle copied his father and opened the moving company that would eventually employ me the box donkey, my stepdad the gear head, and my mom the receptionist. Almost everyone in the family worked there at some point. Yes, it was nepotism, if nepotism means roping your family into jobs where they feel pressured to work unpaid overtime. It certainly had to do with laziness, since none of us ever had to write a resumé. Technically, we were Bed Buggers, a transport industry term that isn't meant to be a compliment.

When I was growing up, my parents and I moved more times than I can count. We bounced from apartment to apartment and never bought a house. If it wasn't because we, as movers, were leading by example, then it was because we chose to spend our money on *things* instead of on a mortgage. We couldn't ignore the two-thousand-dollar vacuum cleaner and its dozen idle tentacles sitting in the corner, the machine that was supposed to huff all our problems up; the marble chess board in a home without any chess players; the banjo that was supposed to turn my stepdad into a bluegrass musician if he would ever pick it up. Our many homes looked like the soundstages on *The Price Is Right*: perpetually filled with new items we couldn't afford. We threw away the packaging as if we wouldn't need it the next time the lease was up. This was in addition to the junk we took in that customers got rid of. There was nowhere to walk. The dripping oil in the goddess rain lamp sure stank, but it was a baroque beauty that didn't belong in the garbage. A mover's house is both a museum to the lives that strangers once lived and to the lives the mover hasn't dared to.

July the first may be Canada Day, but in Quebec it's better known as Moving Day, when most leases start and end and tens of thousands of Montrealers swap not only abodes but also dust mites and plumbing problems. We fight over elevators and parking spots. We complain about the heat, as if doing this dance in the deep freeze of winter would be better. Whatever happens must happen before midnight. Eviction piles litter the sidewalks. It's a season of high tempers but also of heartbreak. In this ludicrous game of musical homes in a quickly gentrifying metropolis, not everyone finds a place to land.

Classic rock kept us going through the sweaty days and nights riding the fleet. "Money for Nothing" by Dire Straits was unofficially known as The Mover's Song for how it referenced installing microwave ovens and colour TVs, a tune the men in my family cranked up whenever it came on the truck radio. I sang along to everything except the line about *the little faggot with the earring*, maybe because I felt it read me too closely.

For whatever reason—perhaps a shiftlessness in my bones that I had learned on the trucks—this wasn't madness enough for me. In 1998, I took a Greyhound from Montreal to New York with only a backpack, intent on reducing the act of moving to its simplest form. I soon found a furnished room in a boarding house in Crown Heights, Brooklyn, and slept on a bed I was destined to forget in a few months. I opened the Yellow Pages, called fifty moving companies, and, a week later, found myself in the warehouse of Urban Moving Systems in Weehawken, New Jersey. So fresh in the city and already part of the bridge-and-tunnel crowd. The Israeli American boss, Dominik, looked me up and down to suss me out.

Can you handle the pressure?

I can work a long day, yeah. That's no problem. I can do three moves in a row if I have to.

That's not what I meant. Where did you say you were from again?

I thought I had already seen it all. To be a mover is to be a keeper of secrets. While packing first drawers, we learn all about a person's sex life. We play anthropologist when we observe the depressions in a mattress and figure out who's been sleeping there. We play psychologist when we listen to customers reassure themselves that they're moving up in the world, not down. It's possible that the furniture doesn't fit, that the hermit crab has clearly chosen the wrong new shell, but we can never let this on. We must use whatever *Tetris* skills we've acquired to complement the image of the life the customer has chosen.

The saddest part of being a mover is seeing people at their lowest points, the invasion of what should be private moments. We try to be discreet because it's the human thing to do. Like the time we found hundreds of empty plastic two-litre Coke bottles covering the apartment floor, including under the bed. The customer looked at us either with a silent apology, a plea for help, or both. There was the guy who visited his storage locker every few days to retrieve personal items. Eventually, we found his wet toothbrush and dirty socks and deduced that he lived there.

Once, mid-move, a customer stabbed himself in the eye with a ballpoint pen; his wife jumped into action and rushed him to the hospital. They came back several hours later, the husband wearing an eyepatch, his cheek encrusted with pus. "I have to do that," he told us, in pain. "I have to give her something else to focus on." Another time, we showed up to move a woman who confided to us that she and her child had to be gone before her husband came home. We understood the stakes and finished in record time; I'm so glad she called us. On jobs like this, it was our duty to smile and pretend not to notice anything, even though we couldn't help it. To be a mover is not merely to witness breakups but to be a part of their machinery.

So what did Dominik mean, *Can you handle the pressure?*

Movers are experts in sensitive home dynamics, and so are doormen, hairdressers, and taxi drivers. In "Mr and Mrs B," Alexander Chee documents his time as a cater-waiter for William F. and Pat Buckley in their Manhattan maisonette, where he remained as invisible as possible in his tailored tuxedo while socialites drank Kir Royales and determined the fate of the city. Chee writes that "being a cater-waiter allowed me access to the interiors of people's lives in a way that was different from every other relationship I might have had. When you're a waiter, clients usually treat you like human furniture. The result is that you see them in unguarded moments, and that, I liked."

I could relate to being treated like human furniture—and, sometimes, as even less valuable than the pieces I was moving. When a customer gave instructions on how to handle an expensive, fragile item, it often felt like they were showing off. *It's nice, right? I paid a lot for it.* We could sense the craving for affirmation and responded accordingly. *So gorgeous. A true one-of-a-kind. We'll take real good care of it.* The subtext was that by comparison, the cost of the move was not a lot of money. And yet, sometimes our tip—for having protected priceless artwork all day—was a handshake and a glass of water.

One December, we arrived at the residence of a former head of state who was paying to send a mostly empty truck to Florida, our only cargo a small mountain of Christmas presents. I remember walking into the basement and seeing the stack of boxes, immaculately wrapped and with matching bows. My friends grew angry when they heard this story, baffled that I didn't sabotage these perfect little environment-destroying Christmases somehow. It was difficult for me to explain that being in someone's house is a sacred trust. When Chee's friends found out he was working for William F.—who once wrote a column suggesting that people with AIDS be tattooed—they called for revenge, ignoring the fact that Chee needed the money and the stability his job provided. "And besides, *he* didn't really matter. I loved *her*," meaning Pat.

When the customers weren't there, the temptation to pretend that these were our houses was great. There's a scene I love in Bong Joon Ho's *Parasite*, a film about the Kims, a poor family who infiltrates the house of the wealthy Park family. The Parks go on a luxury version of a camping trip, and when the Kims find themselves alone in the living room of the mansion in their care, they spread out and drink the finest liqueurs. They end up partially trashing the room, as if the ability to wreck something is the point of owning it.

While I have little in common with the Kim family, I recognize that scene intimately. We movers have held Emmy statuettes, luxuriated in palatial libraries too long, and contemplated Rothko paintings slightly beyond us, and in so doing, inhabited imaginary futures. A violation of trust? I'm not sure. But not everybody had Emmys or Rothkos. It took me a while to realize that some customers were in the same socio-economic positions as we were and just needed their stuff moved at prices they could barely afford.

Regardless of the players, we knew everything about the people we moved, but they knew nothing about us and never asked, even when there was so much to tell. Maybe we movers are to blame for this phenomenon because we like to keep our private lives a secret. Photographers wait for their first solo gallery show so they can ditch the warehouse for the darkroom. Deejays move brownstones to pay for stacks of vinyl heavier than anything they lift with the day stiffs. Novelists rumble over potholes in the back of a truck, hoping to sneak in another scene before an armoire takes them out. For some, it's just a matter of time. For others, the refrain of leaving is one they'll sing for the rest of their lives while carting other people's furniture to places they themselves will never go. This is why Manhattan has the heaviest furniture in the world.

*

It's no coincidence that some of the most displaced people—the ones with no stable homes, or who have houses elsewhere they can't return to—become the ones who professionally uproot others. Many of my colleagues in New York and New Jersey were undocumented: immigrants awaiting status, stranded between countries without money for airfare, separated from their families due to racist security policies, and worse. They came from countries all over, including wealthier ones, which did nothing to lessen their precarity. Sergei had been a practising surgeon in Russia, but his medical degree wasn't recognized in the United States. We called him The Doctor and it made him proud. I'm pretty sure we consulted him about our bumps and sprains, as if inching grand pianos up staircases couldn't explain them.

Johnny had been a soldier in the American War in Vietnam. He often teared up while talking about his combat experiences. His PTSD went unaddressed, and his government failed him on many other levels. One day, Johnny announced he was moving to Tucson with his girlfriend. They were going to pack and load all their stuff and drive the rental truck themselves. He spoke of Arizona in riddles and referred to it as a panacea, as if another crappy moving job wasn't awaiting him on the other side of the four-day drive.

Many of my colleagues were Black men whose experiences with racism I witnessed first-hand every day. When Kevin ran jobs, people mistakenly assumed his white coworkers were in charge. When Tony had trouble breaking a hundred in the city for lunch, we broke it for him and cursed the lunch counters. Comparatively, my privileges were immense. I'm white. Yes, I had moved to New York with no prospects and very little money, and, with cash so short, I was financially beholden to my employers. I was working "illegally" and was vulnerable for other reasons. Still, I grew up in a moving company and could always leverage that experience. I could return home to Canada if I really had to.

Regardless of a mover's circumstances, their body is always a cushion. I was there the day Johnny Five (yes, a different Johnny) was schlepping an industrial metal sink down a staircase and let a corner crush his knee against a wall rather than drop it. My buddy Paul was once knocked unconscious by a falling ramp and had to take months of unpaid time off work to recover from a concussion. Eventually, everyone succumbs to repetitive strain injury. It's rare for a relocation company—aside from the major van lines—to offer health insurance to its staff, or even training to help them avoid throwing out their backs.

The pandemic, a time when we're all supposed to reduce travel and contact, has conversely led to more moves, most of them unplanned. Don't worry, movers can handle the overflow, and they feel most comfortable when you're all swapping zip codes. But Covid-19 poses new risks to them, many of whom already suffer chronic health conditions related to their job. I have asthma, which was surely made worse—if not caused—by years of breathing in dust from packing paper and the bottoms of a thousand closets. How can a mover "reduce contact" when a mattress is pressed to their face? What would happen to the American Dream if all movers everywhere quit on the same day? How many elevator shafts would be plugged up with the waste product of our consumer impulses? How long before we realize capitalism is no longer portable and society unravels even further?

I want everyone to agree that it's better to dent a sink than to break a kneecap.

*

We were somewhere in the Garden State, perhaps between tailing ponds and the turnpike, when I learned the definition of pressure that Dominik had hinted at. We had just arrived at a customer's house to do a long-distance move charged by the pound. Andris, the foreman, winked at us, and said to watch what he does and learn from it. He rang the bell, the customer answered, and we all walked in. Andris looked around and threw his arms in the air.

Wow, so much stuff. We had no idea.

What do you mean? the customer said. *I told you exactly what I have.*

Clearly not. This is going to be overweight.

But you already gave me an estimate.

It was non-binding. Listen. I can help you out. It will be cheaper if we do it for a fixed price. (Thinks up a number.) *X should cover it.*

Thank you so much!

Of course, X ended up being more.

There are so many other scams. If you're charged by the cubic foot, you could end up paying for fifty empty boxes. Jobs by the hour can mysteriously take forever. If you're charged by the pound and don't fall for a fixed price, the movers might use fuel, hidden shipments, or their own bodies to tip the scales. The final price is miles from the estimate. If you don't pay the overage, they could simply put the furniture in storage until you do, which only drives the cost higher. Your dreams are now being held hostage in a warehouse piled with the dreams of strangers, each indistinguishable from the next. Whether you buy insurance or count on the one that comes free, there won't be a damage payout if the inventory sheet already lists the piece in question as being "worn" or "used," which is often the case. When you sign the contract, you might be agreeing to several hidden charges you never bothered to check: ten bucks for a roll of tape, seventy-five to unscrew the two bolts in a bed frame. Most surcharges are perfectly legal, but it doesn't mean they're *legit*.

I can tell you all this now because I'm no longer a mover. "Waiters and escorts both know that indiscretion is a career-ending move," Chee writes. "You only reveal a secret if you are never going back again."

Sometimes it's not the movers' fault. Customers can downplay how much furniture they have, omit the six flights of stairs, or forget to book the elevator. They might say everything will be pre-packed, only for movers to find shelves and cabinets still loaded with stuff. Movers are often blamed for a customer's lack of preparation or understanding of what moving entails. It can be a failure of empathy.

Or a moving company might pressure staff to make as much money as possible as a condition of keeping their jobs. I've seen foremen balk at applying surcharges, only to have the boss scream at them over the phone and override any sense of fairness. It can also be the opposite: a greedy foreman can go rogue unbeknownst to the company. Regardless of how the scams play out, they ultimately put vulnerable movers at risk. The customers call the police and we—the people who became or remained movers to avoid interacting with authorities—must explain disputes to them.

Most of the companies I worked for were honest and didn't pull these scams. We talked openly about the tricks and advised customers on how to protect themselves. But it was different at Urban Moving. When I saw foremen squeeze people for money in their own homes, I cringed, but I also didn't do much to stop it, which is something I have to live with.

I remember the day I hit my limit. It wasn't even the day dispatch shooed us out of the warehouse in the morning with little information or time to stock up on necessary equipment, so that we went to Ithaca—Ithaca!—without enough boxes to pack the thousands of books the customer had, or dollies to push them on.

No, it was another fifteen-hour day that did it. I was finally made foreman, an honour I didn't want, but one that Dominik thought I could, and should, carry. We were moving an apartment in Jersey City on a job charged by the hour. I had no interest in scamming—I just wanted it not to end in disaster, like so many moves did. But the day quickly went sideways despite my best efforts; we had underestimated the distance from the parking lot to the lobby to the elevator to the hallway to the apartment. The customer's father-in-law accused us of dragging our asses to inflate the cost. By the time I admitted to the customer that I couldn't figure out how to disassemble the wall unit, tensions peaked; by the time the driver got stuck in the parking lot—he had wedged the truck impossibly between a Mercedes and a retaining wall—the father-in-law had had it. *I'm calling the Jersey City PD!* He did, they came, but there was nothing to do except change drivers and try to shimmy past the Mercedes. When the day finally ended a year later, we drove back to the warehouse in the middle of the night, starving, exhausted, and fighting with each other. The crew was furious with me because I hadn't managed to score a tip beyond a glass of water for them.

For me, that was it. I walked into Dominik's office that week and told him I wanted to leave, which I feared he could make complicated by bringing up my visa situation.

You're not happy here?

No, not really. I'm going to work for a company in Manhattan. It's closer. No offense.

You're one hundred percent free to go, he told me with a look I'll never forget. *There's no one stopping you. You can do whatever you want.*

It was a weird thing to say. I was grateful, but also a bit disappointed at how expendable I was, the proof that there's so little that anchors movers, we who anchor everything. I was certain I'd never hear of the company again.

When the Twin Towers came down two years later, on September 11, 2001, I was in Montreal, watching on TV what I knew was a cross between mass death and the single greatest displacement of furniture in the modern world. What I didn't know—until many more years later—was that that morning, a resident of an apartment complex in Union City, New Jersey, saw three employ-ees of Urban Moving photographing the burning towers from the roof of their empty van and, in her estimation, celebrating. She notified the authorities, and the FBI promptly arrested the movers; Dominik and his family fled the country mere days later. What would become five suspects—whom I didn't know—were held and interrogated for two months on suspicion of espionage, and everything in the abandoned Weehawken ware-house went back to its rightful owners. Even though all parties would later be exonerated, the anti-Semitic conspiracy theory of the "Five Dancing Israelis"—who had advance knowledge of 9/11 but withheld it to boost sympathy for Israel—would persist for decades. Eventually, Donald Trump, the mangler-in-chief, would twist the story into something even more improbable: the five Israelis became "thousands and thousands" of Muslims in New Jersey cheering the attacks. Others have written about this in greater detail; this is not that essay.

Besides, I don't need to tell you why someone might react to an overturned skyline by photographing it, or why shock might look like celebration to someone watching from a distance on a panic-filled morning, or why a family might hop a plane when the xenophobia of millions suddenly turns on them. Urban Mov-ing was no front; the truth is that it was just another poorly run moving outfit that exploited customers for a quick buck. In my view, the scams, ironically, are what exonerate the company: no competent spy agency would willingly risk so many run-ins with the cops. I couldn't have spent eight months at the heart of a covert intelligence cell and missed it; it was, on the contrary, the most disorganized group of people I've ever known. My former boss, who once appeared on an FBI 9/11 suspect list but is now in California working in new lines of business, has never publicly commented on the story. To those who find his silence incriminating, I'll reiterate what I've been saying all along: for many, to survive even a day in the United States means keeping their mouths shut.

None of this should be surprising. In the US, as in Canada, undocumented workers are supposed to take the blame. In 2001, you couldn't hold a surveillance camera without arousing suspicion unless you were a white citizen, and that is very likely still the case. Colonial and imperial powers become enraged when others dare to record history through their own lenses. To some, there's nothing more intimidating than an empty van. They don't see their furniture inside, and it's just another reminder that they're not going anywhere. More than that, the empty space hints at the death of consumerism. It's the terrifying suggestion that we don't have more refrigerators than we have trucks to carry them; that our appetites just might exceed the supply of what we crave and that we could go hungry. Capitalism has taught us to fear a broken supply chain more than death itself.

*

Being a mover changes how you see the world. When the curtain comes down at the theatre, you can't enjoy the intermission because you're too busy thinking about the stagehands striking the set and if they're paid well enough. When a family is moving on a TV show, it's obvious to you if the boxes stacked around them are empty; the suggestion is that your profession isn't worth making look believable. You can't remember how many people you told that *Taxi* was originally supposed to be about movers until the producers decided you were uninteresting.

I may have gotten out of the biz, but I'm a lifer at heart. I always answer the call when a friend needs help moving. I tighten the hump strap, seal boxes tape-to-tape, and put my creaking back into it. The few times I've hired movers, I've been so keen to join the crews, they've had to forcibly remove me from the truck. I tip them inappropriately high amounts, as if I must atone for the sins of cheapskates everywhere.

I don't know if Johnny ever made it to Tucson, or if Sergei ever worked as a surgeon again.

What I know is that any story a mover tells has fallen off the back of a truck. The story revolves around the imperfect edges of a *thing*, one that fits a hole in their life. You'll hear about this thing eventually, and for the hundredth time, but not for the final time. The story might be about how this thing saved them, and how they can't live without it. This is the real mover's song. And it could be literally anything: a juniper-wood banjo, loose ball bearings, splinters that smell like mint but aren't toothpicks, hood ornaments for extinct cars, medals from unspecified wars, a petrified wedding cake, toys over-loved, a crystal ashtray chipped down to a star, a livid scorpion trapped in amber, a nude jazz record, a tent repair kit, a teak coffee table in the shape of a guitar pick, a Polaroid of a deck of cards, a CD autographed with a styptic pencil, a trailer hitch wearing a scarf of baby's breath, a wine decanter from Jericho, a subway token from before the inevitable fall of Manhattan.

But none of these things can be yours.

Our fingerprints are on everything, so while we can be blamed for it all, the world also belongs to us.

Acadia Currah

///////

FEMME FATALES AND THE LAVENDER MENACE

Love is Julia Roberts's teeth, head thrown back in laughter over something male lead number three has said. It's a strong hand fitting over the curve of a narrow waist. A dip, a look, a tip-toe kiss. It's always "Falling" in love: Freefall, no parachute, blind trust. Nobody tells you to break into love, how to be in-bobby-pin-between-your-teeth slipping-gift-cards-through-door-hinges love. How to have an invisible laurel of blood-bruise kisses pressing thorns into the crown of your head, tangling your hair. How to be sealed like a letter, deep red like a brand.

She sits behind you in science class, eyes a wet-denim blue. You snap little rubber bands on your wrists until they burn raw and red. Two snaps for staring. Three if she catches you. You say no when she asks you to get lunch, say you aren't hungry.

But you are.

You're in the library together, and she's looking at you. "This one's my favourite." So you dog-ear your bible and learn something else.

And your mother always hated your table manners, said you ate like you were afraid someone would take it from you. You think that's how you love too. You carry it like a wound, hold your hand over it and pretend you can't feel the sticky warmth running between your fingers. You're, a little bit, like a child playing hide-and-seek, standing out in the open with your eyes closed. "If I can't see you, you can't see me."

It's all pointless anyway, because you don't even like girls. You wear that belief like a watch, like a compass, using it as a constant reorientation of who you are. Whenever you find yourself too closely watching her clip her hair back, it's two snaps and "I don't like girls." Apply the words like pressure on a fresh cut, pull them tight and wrap them til you can't see red.

You learn how to do a lockstitch across your chest, how to tie it up like a bow; you cannot breathe too heavily, too deep, or it'll snap.

When you were nine, you trekked to the end of your very long driveway to school, waited for the yellow bus. Ottawa winters are bitterly, unforgivably cold; your walk was separated into long stretches of shade and sparse patches of sunlight. Whenever you'd feel the sun hit your face, you'd imagine it soaking into your skin, walk like you had heavy sunshine bowls on your shoulders, careful not to spill any warmth. Not until you needed to use it, not until the cold stuck two inches deep, made your knees feel stale-bread crackable. Then, you'd dip your hands into heat storage, let it boil over until you stepped onto the bus, eyes scouring for a window seat. You never got one.

She's flashing you an under-the-eyelashes smile, and you feel something familiar fill on your shoulders, feel something sink in your gut.

You can't like girls anyway. Because if love feels like someone's kicked the door in on your heart and rearranged all the furniture in your bedroom, and there's nothing to be done, because nothing has been stolen; it's only, horribly, jarringly different . . . If love feels like that, you do not want it.

You don't like girls, because if you did, you would have to look different. You're fourteen, and they tell you the curve of your hips and waist are too big, too soft, to be for anything other than a boy's hungry hands. They tell you that you are shaped like sex. You can't like girls. Because girls' hands are too small, they could never touch you correctly, not in the way you're meant to be touched. Not hard and heavy and dark. You're an hourglass, a Coke bottle. You are meant to be cracked.

You're at a sleepover, and they're asking "Who do you like?" all fuck-marry-killing and truth or dare. You feel ready to split, crack open to the moulding marrow of your heart. You shrug, "Dustin, probably."

You picked him because he has soft-looking hair and shiny braces. Later, he passes you a note in the chapel saying he likes you too. You nod, bless yourself backwards, try to ignore the panic rising in your chest, hot and acidic.

And they tell you love should make your heart softer, open it like a too-tight pickle-jar lid. She paints purple-black onto your eyes, and a "You look pretty." And your heart is a mango pit; you think you'd need a special tool to open it, sweet, fleshy fruit around it. Hard, unforgiving.

You're fourteen when you hear the word. "Dyke." It's not the way you'd use it now, not in a fierce redemption, it's a spat "Fucking bull-dyke." And you feel defensive, embarrassed. It doesn't make sense because you like boys. You couldn't be the black-leather-jacket buzz-cut-girl they're talking about, the one with skinny jeans at tattoo arms. You're soft, and the word burns into your chest. You want to make something tangible and rip it with your bit-nail hands. You swallow it like a multi-vitamin, the same way you take the belief that it could not, ever, be you.

You wear pink sweatshirts and tight jeans, all high-ponytails and a please-don't-look-at-me pair of black-framed glasses. You play Taylor Swift and dutifully listen when she instructs you to shake it off. You can't like girls; you're pretty, all your friends are girls. You can't like girls, because you're scared of boys, and if your friends were scared of you like that, you wouldn't know what to do.

So you plant a Lip Smacker kiss on a boy's cheek, run your hands over his arms. Ignore the way he looks at you, hungry, wanting. Ignore the way it makes your stomach turn.

Everyone knows boys have shark teeth, glinting under street-lights you shouldn't be out long enough to see turn on. You are worried the way you look at her will take a file to your mouth, sharpening flat into threatening. And you know, more than any-thing, that you love like a girl, that you hold people warm inside your body. You know it when she tucks her head into your shoul-der, and you hold your breath, making it comfortable, trying to soften tense muscle. You know you love like a shapeshifter, that you'd be her pillow and footstool and oven. You can be her best friend and makeup artist and Border Collie, but you cannot be her boyfriend.

Boys get the window seat, shoulder their way through and in. You knock on her doors with a basket of cinnamon buns, know-ing that she'll only ever let you in through the trap door, the one down the back alley. You know you'll go anyway, shove all your hair up into a baseball cap the way she wants you to, just happy to be out of the cold. Leave the basket out front anyway, steaming and ready.

You're sixteen, and you meet somebody else. She has pink hair and glittery eyeliner and calls herself "Femme." You think it's short for feminine. She rolls her eyes when you say it. "It's different," she replies and refuses to elaborate. And "Why do you care so much anyway?"

Why do you care so much anyway?

She's beautiful, not clean or classical. She has big tacky earrings, unshaved legs, choppy, faded-dye hair, big black boots, and a purple eyeshadow glare.

She's looking at you like she's seeing past everything you've been trying frantically to hide, pushing walls down like a Jenga tower.

And you don't love her. Not in that way. But she's stomping you around downtown pointing out rainbow flags in every window, and "I met my ex-girlfriend there one time" and telling you Doc Martens would "Totally match that whole thing you have going on."

"What whole thing?" you ask, and she looks at you like she sees the child with her eyes closed out in the open, the one with the bent-up bible and frozen fingers. She shrugs, "Never mind."

And you meet her friends, all dyed and ripped jackets and patches on their backpacks. The one with an eyebrow piercing offers to read your tarot. You will have great luck with money and love.

It's not a church, because there's no stained glass and straight-back pews. But when she feeds you a stale Dorito, it hits your tongue like communion bread, her shitty unmixed original song like a hymn.

She likes your ripped tights; you meet leather vest girls, red lipstick boys. You trade your heavy black frames for gold wire-rims, swap your baseball cap for pink hair clips. You still stare, but you take off the rubber band, still feel the phantom sting sometimes.

And you like girls.

Sadiqa de Meijer

DO NO HARM

I went to medical school in a prison town. At first the Kingston prisons seemed to me like the sugar refineries or steel plants of other cities, simply the main local industry. One of them—a grey, neoclassical, walled compound—was near the campus, on the lake. Another, across from the Value Village, resembled a small castle with red spires; some locals called it Disneyland North. There were four other major institutions outside the city, much less visible from the road.

Some students joked about them. These tended to be young white men who, if they ever did find themselves in jail, would likely soon be freed through family connections, or a judge who saw himself reflected in their faces, their manner, or their home address. It was new for me to be around classmates like that—ones who might play a round of golf with the dean or department head, hired housekeepers, and shopped at thrift stores only satirically, at Halloween. In their company, the feminist and anti-corporate perspectives that I'd come to take for granted as a campus activist at the University of Western Ontario were considered amusing, though amusement was only the waxy coating over a compressed sense of entitlement; if I pushed through, I knew there would be contempt, and even fury.

When it came to prisons, however, I had nothing to say; my life at the turn of the millennium had afforded me that ignorance. While my parents had modest incomes, they also had graduate degrees. The racisms I'd encountered were particular to being perceived as mixed race, or South Asian, or Arabic. They were not anti-Black or anti-Indigenous, and therefore did not place me at exponentially higher risk of imprisonment. I saw the prisons as ominous boxes, self-contained and arbitrarily situated in our area. Their relationship to the community remained obscure.

Then, during the first month of classes, I volunteered for an after-school arts program at a local public school. I worked with first-graders who had been identified in evasive professional language as *at risk*. One afternoon, around a low, rectangular table strewn with pipe cleaners and Popsicle sticks, one grim little girl in pigtails told me that her father was a trucker and gone all the time. Immediately, three or four other children claimed the same.

I brought up this coincidence with their teacher afterwards, and she clarified that the fathers were incarcerated. Although I can't recall what the teacher looked like, in my memory she struck that common tone in which the initiated speak to relative outsiders about prisons—or perhaps in which we respond to any privileged innocence—with a degree of pleasure at its erasure. In return, I made an effort to hide my dismay. And what do we do that for? I mean assimilate terrible facts by pretending not to feel.

My privilege had classist and racist foundations, and somehow caused me to underestimate the love in the lives of imprisoned people. I had pictured men—the downtown prison was a men's institution—without relations, and failed to consider that their partners and children and mothers would move to live near them, for the sake of whatever contact was allowed. It was a subtraction I had made from their humanity. If my own father or brothers were long-term prisoners, I, too, would try to make visits affordable and practical. My privilege was that this circumstance seemed unimaginable. I stood nearer, in other words, to the fraternity men of my class than I had realized.

My sense of immunity would soon undergo an adjustment. I started medical school in 2001, and September 11 was our second day of classes. During an early break, a fellow student appeared at the lectern and said she had just read at the library's computer terminal that America was under attack. Our class stirred in disbelief and confusion, but the next professor took the stage without comment, and the title of his PowerPoint presentation appeared on the screen: Blood. I listened for a few minutes, saw that the material was familiar, and left to get the news. During the months and years after that, as an anti-terrorist infrastructure was taking shape to target people who resembled us, I would learn to worry for my brothers and their possible incarceration. I would finally grasp that, for many, prison gates were only a crooked official or bureaucratic error away.

Back in that public school classroom, however, the aches of those six-year-olds were a revelation. Afterwards, whenever I passed the prison, I could almost see their love and longing and anger for their fathers, tethered and drifting from the razor-wired walls like threads of spider silk.

*

The next impression the prisons made on me was an indirect but gruesome one. As part of our medical training, we were each required to shadow a paramedic team for one shift. I told my friend and classmate I had spent a quiet evening eating doughnuts and watching comedies at the station, and responding to a single call from a woman with back pain. The paramedics were relaxed as she limped from her house to the ambulance; she was a regular, they said. Then I asked my friend about his experience.

He was usually wryly funny. He explained that his team had been called to the downtown prison after a suicide. They had to cut a hanging man down. His voice was both incredulous and already imbued with a determined acceptance, as if he took it as his duty to withstand what he had witnessed.

*

Then came the clinical years.

"I have lunch at twelve," a tall, thin patient in the infectious disease clinic told me. He repeated this several times as I persisted in a thorough assessment.

"You're meeting someone for lunch?" I asked.

"No," he said, looking at me with scorn, "I'm in prison."

The placid man in the waiting room—his partner or friend, I had assumed—must have been a guard.

The term "minimum security" occurred to me. The question of what he had done. *Never ask them that* was the only instruction I ever heard from a professor regarding prisoner patients.

*

As hospital admissions, prisoners were marked with a middle initial of "X" on our lists. I suppose this was to alert health-care workers to potential complications: the impossibility of a neuro-logical exam on a person in shackles or the need to allow a guard into the imaging room. The prisoner in-patients were people twice institutionalized. I wondered if the hospital was a respite for them.

One night, I was called to a ward room with two uniformed guards at its doors. There were four patients inside—three in the usual half-curtained beds, and one man on a gurney in the aisle. I had his chart in my hands. Restraints locked his wrists and ankles to the rails, and were impossible to reconcile with his condition; he was emaciated, fevered, and trembling. We were approximately the same age. His diagnoses were pneumonia, diabetes, and HIV/AIDS, and I could see from his bloodwork that he was critically ill.

"I'm all right," he kept telling me in a small voice fractured with pain, "I think it's just a cold." He had big, dark eyes. I told myself that he had probably been violent—and that he would trick me, too, if required, easily and remorselessly, in a habitual fight for survival. I did that, I now see, because of the vulnerabil-ity I perceived in him, which dwelled momentarily at his surface It made me want to stay and hold his hand, but I knew that doing so would cost me, in some unwritten sense, as a medical student; we were supposed to be tougher than that.

The next prisoner I remember was a bearded, red-haired man lying handcuffed to a gurney in a hallway, awaiting surgery. It was another incongruous picture. Pre-operative patients already seem disarmed: they lack their usual clothing, or their eyesight, or the sense of remove from their own mortality. The man's restraints, in this context, implied that the threat he posed was immense.

There was also the strange sequence of procedures that had been or would be done to his body: immobilization by chains, and then by anaesthesia; cutting and cauterizing; leaks of blood. Their meanings blurred, and the rituals of surgery could suddenly be perceived as punitive, or even as a curing of whatever was amiss in him, the ablation of the will to harm.

*

These mental images of corrective procedures now strike me as central to the incarceration system's own unsettled question: Should inmates be punished or rehabilitated? Isolation is already inherently painful to our nature. Past that punishing aspect, doing time is not a blank, suspended existence, and the condition of people released from prisons depends on the substance of their days, months, and years of incarceration.

The doctor at one of the clinics I rotated through also worked inside the prisons. When I asked about his experience, he told me how disastrous it was that prisoners could not clean their needles for drug use. He had advocated for bleach buckets on the range, the common area directly outside the cells, but those were deemed too dangerous. He described a horrific economy, in which some prisoners would swallow their prescribed medications under supervision, then make themselves vomit to sell the pills. The money might be for food, phone calls, or contraband. He seemed to speak with an extinguished kindness, in a sandpaper voice.

I think of the efforts made by doctors, or teachers, or other institutional workers, to not feel too much. If the purpose of prisons was truly rehabilitation, that numbing practice would have no place. The buildings would have to be architecturally overhauled, their interiors no longer resembling cages. Instead of infrequent and opaque reports of an inmate death, a riot, or a drone ferrying contraband over a wall, we would hear regularly from incarcerated people themselves. They would receive a dignified rate of pay for their labour.

Contemporary prisons are supposed to have classrooms and libraries and culturally oriented anger management programs, measures intended to lead to the release of benign and skilled individuals. But what I've observed of people on day parole, on statutory release, or in resumed lives of relative freedom, is that living in prison has left signs of trauma: scars, restlessness, a vigilant scanning of the periphery. Correctional officers, too, are affected by the institutions; a recent Canadian study found that more than a third suffer from work-related PTSD. When human exchanges are fraught with threat, mistrust, or abuse, no one involved is immune.

*

Kingston's historic downtown prison closed in 2013, and three years later it reopened for tourism. I went on a bright day one May, a decade after I had left both the hospital and medicine itself. I wanted to know what was inside the walls that I had passed by hundreds of times.

Two young students guided our group through the family visiting rooms, where microphones were embedded in the small, metal tables, and past the domed, central space with its tiered ranges, inside the metal workshops, and along a row of open cells. Under the dome was a panoptical guard station, a geometric structure of steel and bullet-proof glass. There were framed pictures on the wall. One photograph from the 1970s showed the inmates relaxed and crowded along the fenced galleries, listening to a live concert.

At each stop, retired Kingston Penitentiary officers told us the history of what we were viewing. Some seemed to offer a straightforward perspective. One former guard with a booming voice recalled the period when officer weapons were stored beneath the guard post: "Having the armoury here was wonderful. We could get anything we needed. Pistols, guns, gas, batons, shields." A stern woman described doing cell checks: "We looked for a live, breathing body."

Other narrators used forms of doublespeak that I couldn't quite decipher. A gaunt man with a moustache said smilingly, "When we got the security cameras in, the prisoners really liked that." *The undesirables*, others said, or *the definition of reasonable force*. The tour was strictly timed and surveilled; whenever I lingered at a stop to ask questions, one of the students would return and rush me through the tight and labyrinthine hallways after the group.

I thought of Charles Dickens's description of the place in 1842. He was travelling through eastern America and Canada, making stops in Boston, Toronto, and Niagara Falls. Of Kingston, he wrote: "There is an admirable jail here, well and wisely governed, and excellently regulated, in every respect." At the time, some inmates were children under the age of ten, routinely whipped for breaking rules that included not speaking or giggling.

What felt cumulative, during our tour of the now dormant building, was the effect of endless cold, hard surfaces—metal, limestone, and concrete—ubiquitous in the floors, the walls, the bars, the railings, the seats, the tables, the bunks. Everything was made to withstand force or to be hosed down, but people had lived there—breathing bodies—and I saw no means for them to be even fleetingly at ease. The punishment or rehabilitation question seemed settled in the furnishings themselves.

There was, even as we walked the extensive outdoor grounds, a sense of suffocation rising in me. Where were the former prisoners' voices? In the segregation unit, where a residual atmosphere of suffering remained unmistakable, I saw a skilled drawing of an Indigenous Medicine Wheel, along with axes, a feather, and a grieving woman's face, still on the cinderblock wall of a cell.

*

We were not supposed to ask, at the hospital, what a prisoner had done because the answer could affect our duty to provide impartial care. This is a beautiful principle in medicine: the idea that every wound deserves the same quality of attention, no matter who bears it. But what we were more implicitly taught not to pursue is the question of where the injury began. With a famine; a slave ship; a broken treaty; with the Sixties Scoop.

Some months after the tour, I was at a community meeting that involved a sharing circle. One of those present was a muscular white man with a tense demeanour. In the circle, he volunteered that he had done what he called the worst thing possible, and had served his time. He was frustrated that many people—potential employers, friends, or lovers—still saw him as a criminal. "What about forgiveness?" he asked.

He sat beside me, and we were without the separations that institutions impose—without the white coat and the orange jumpsuit, the scripted roles of authority and compliance. He spoke with a volatile impatience. Ideologically, I wanted to agree with his perspective, to erase the weight of his past, but instinctively, I wanted only to be less near him, and to not mention that I had a daughter. The fault wasn't mine or his, but collective; my sense, bodily and trusted, was that whatever had happened to him in the name of justice and rehabilitation had not worked. I don't believe prisons enclose or remediate physically violent behaviour. They are a stopover in its circuits, where pain and trauma are amplified.

Activist movements for prison reform or abolition are more prominent now than they were when I was a student, but perhaps what requires reform first is our definition of what constitutes violence. At the after-school arts program, many of the children gathered around that glue-stained crafting table— who aren't children now, who probably have children of their own—were chronically hungry, and to be six years old and hungry in a city of stocked stores, among gleaming billboard images of restaurant meals, is violence; to be a mother with only a few dollars of grocery money per day is violence; for a child to name their hunger to the wrong adult and lose their family is violence.

That genocide is violence goes without saying; its brutal aftermath marks communities for generations. Living with a pervasive cultural image of yourself as inferior is also violence, and when the police and courts base their work on that image, the system becomes an entrapment.

In relation to those forms of violence, most of us accord ourselves a false sense of blamelessness. We don't determine rates for social assistance programs; we don't refuse to fund water filtration systems for Indigenous communities; we don't fasten the handcuffs to the stretcher. Our own violence takes the form of silent, continuous consent; it lives in us, a negative space with armoured walls.

After the prison tour, I remembered another way that the prisons had come up during our first week of med school: the downtown penitentiary was rumoured to house Paul Bernardo, a serial rapist who also murdered three girls. My cohort was the same generation as his teenage victims, and it was natural that we would discuss him—but now I also see the implications of us naming only that inmate, one who was monstrous, and undoubtedly guilty, and could never be safely released. Very few such people exist, but it was convenient to consider him the representative prisoner, because it absolved us of asking who else was in there and what their stories might be. Viewed in the slanted sunlight that makes threads visible—gleaming filaments strung between razor wires and walls—these stories are ones in which we are all complicit. Those hard and unforgiving surfaces are ours.

Gabrielle Drolet

IN DEFENSE OF
GARLIC IN A JAR

How Food Snobs Almost Ruined My Love of Cooking

I was in my second year of university when I discovered the joy of making meals from scratch. My desire to cook was sparked, partly, by the sheer excitement of having access to a kitchen. After a year of mostly eating the same few vegetarian meals from a dorm cafeteria, the possibilities now felt endless. Between classes, I rushed home and delighted in the ritual of trying a new technique or recipe: the perfect temperature at which to roast cauliflower, how to fry tofu so the edges were just crispy enough, how to use up all those cans of chickpeas I bought on sale.

My curiosity was further bolstered by the fact that I was coming into young adulthood around the same time that YouTube cooking channels were becoming part of pop culture; this was 2017, when *Bon Appétit* had just launched its now-famous *Gourmet Makes* series, and shows like *Binging with Babish* were garnering millions of views. As a terminally online student, I spent far too much of my time watching their videos and experimenting with their recipes.

One afternoon, I was making a stir-fry in the small kitchen of a house where I lived. As vegetables sputtered in hot oil on the stove, I remember one of my roommates coming downstairs and poking her head into the kitchen.

"What smells so good?" She smiled.

"Probably the garlic," I answered, stirring the bright contents of the pan.

I recall her eyeing the mess I'd made on the counter—discarded pieces of carrot and onion, spices spilled from plastic bags—and stopping when she saw the little jar. A spoon lay beside it, still slick with preservative oil.

"You use the pre-minced stuff?"

"Yeah," I said.

She wrinkled her nose and receded. I could tell I'd done something unsavoury.

I'd been in the habit of buying jarred garlic—the kind that comes minced and suspended in oil—because it was easy to use. I was still getting accustomed to the patience and time that cooking required, and the jarred stuff seemed like a no-brainer: a way to save a few minutes. But, after that day, I stopped buying it. I'm not sure I even finished that container—it likely sat half-empty in the fridge for the rest of the semester. As I started to pride myself on my cooking, I also became hyperaware of wanting to do things the right way, and I noticed all the recipes and cooking shows I followed only ever used fresh ingredients.

Online, people affirmed my new belief. They joked that those who use jarred garlic can't cook. "What if you met your soul mate, but then found out they cook with pre-minced garlic in a jar," one tweet said. Media outlets published article after article condemning the stuff. An old quote by the celebrity chef Anthony Bourdain seemed to resurface every few months. "Avoid at all costs that vile spew you see rotting in oil in screwtop jars," he had written in his book *Kitchen Confidential*, first published in 2000. "Too lazy to peel fresh? You don't deserve to eat garlic."

This was the first of many haughty ideas I'd hear about cooking and how selective we should be with our food. Who would buy a bottle of lemon juice when you could buy fresh lemons? Shredded cheese when you could grate your own? Pre-sliced mushrooms when they were apparently cheaper and better whole? An image of pre-peeled oranges from Whole Foods caused so much outrage in 2016 that the product was pulled from stores. Then there was the notion that those who opted for these packaged foods or ingredients weren't just lazy—they were wreaking havoc on the environment with all that unnecessary plastic. Under all of this criticism, there was always a minority voice telling people they were being ableist. Those voices reminded us that disabled people rely on these shortcuts—that not everyone can chop and peel and slice. Over and over again, those voices were drowned out by the majority.

I, too, ignored them, and I learned to love fresh garlic. I learned to love the feeling of smashing a clove between a cutting board and the flat side of a knife. Of mincing it: always by hand, never with a press. I learned to always use more than the recipe called for, to love the smell and sizzle of it frying, to make sure it didn't get all browned and bitter in the pan. I learned to appreciate the slight (but usually unnoticeable) difference in taste when I used the fresh stuff, the allicin edge a little sharper or more present.

Then, in early 2021, I developed a nerve problem that changed everything.

*

My life became immeasurably different last winter. A repetitive strain injury led me to develop thoracic outlet syndrome. Pain shot through my forearms and into my fingers when I did simple tasks. My hands often went numb. My elbows ached and seized. Looking down at anything—a book, a cutting board—hurt my neck and shoulders and worsened the rest of my symptoms.

As months went by, I got used to assistive technology, swapping a keyboard for voice-to-text. I asked for help when I needed to. I used paper plates, as I was unable to wash dishes myself. So many things tied to my identity were now inaccessible to me: hobbies such as embroidery and video games, writing with a pen, the Sunday-morning pastime of sitting hunched over a crossword puzzle, filling in and erasing answers. I felt I had lost so much. I didn't want to lose being a good cook too. So I continued to only ever use fresh garlic.

On a good day, I would wince and tear up as I peeled each clove from its papery skin, as I crushed it on a cutting board, as I minced it into tiny pieces. On a bad day, my hands would be so numb and my fingers so swollen that I would be unable to even grip the handle of a knife tightly enough.

Even at such points, I never considered buying jarred garlic. I pushed through the pain, no matter how excruciating. And, on especially bad days, I omitted the ingredient altogether, my food missing a certain edge I'd grown to love.

*

Cooking shortcuts have been around for a long time, but for at least a century, we've been finding ways to appease those who turn their noses up at easier options. In 1929, molasses manufacturer P. Duff & Sons started selling dehydrated flour mix—made up of wheat flour, molasses, sugar, shortening, salt, baking soda, ginger, cinnamon, and powdered whole egg. Housewives simply had to add water to the mixture and bake it to produce a dessert. In the early 1930s, the company released a cake mix with a similar concept. But it later amended the product to have cooks add the eggs themselves, stating, "The housewife and the purchasing public in general seem to prefer fresh eggs." Other food brands, such as Betty Crocker, followed suit.

The fresh eggs did make for a better-tasting dessert—the dried-egg mixtures produced cakes that stuck to the pan and often had a strong flavour of eggs—but the desire to add the ingredient yourself was at least partially psychological. Cracking and mixing in eggs provided the illusion of participation, and this became the first step in making a creation with layers and packaged frosting.

It seems the aesthetics of being a good cook by using fresh ingredients have always triumphed over convenience. But the disdain for shortcuts and anything that isn't fresh feels especially pronounced today. This might be partially because of the wellness industry: as a love of whole foods and a fear of preservatives have become commonplace, people seem more comfortable announcing their disgust for anything processed or impure. Social media has made it easier for fresh-food purists, many with entire accounts devoted to "clean eating," to make their opinions known too. Though not all of these accounts explicitly condemn processed foods, they perpetuate the idea that whole foods are significantly better.

The culture that surrounds cooking today is one that lends itself well to casual ableism. It's a culture that prizes specific ways of doing things over others, constantly pitting methods and recipes against one another: French-style scrambled eggs over American, minced garlic instead of pressed, nonstick pans against those made of cast iron, bouillon cubes against broth cartons against homemade stock. It's a culture desperate to identify serious cooks as opposed to casual ones, assigning value to almost everything we do in the kitchen. Did you stir that with a wooden spoon? Did you cook it in the right kind of oil? Did you use pre-ground pepper? Kosher salt or iodized? In a culture obsessed with the right and wrong way of doing things, any choice you make is likely controversial to some, eliciting either eye rolls or enthusiasm.

Often, the wrong choice is the easier (read: more accessible) one—and making it is a fatal flaw. These aren't things to try to avoid when you can. They're things you should never do, even though many of us don't have a choice. This lack of nuance is what made me believe using accessibility tools might make me a bad cook, pushing me to hurt myself even when cooking alone.

None of this is intentional. People aren't thinking about disabled cooks when they turn their noses up at pre-minced garlic or pre-ground pepper or whatever else. That's part of the problem, though: dismissing ingredients and disparaging anyone who uses them means not thinking of who, exactly, that might be. In reality, it doesn't take much critical thinking to get there.

Who needs to use a quicker, less-labour-intensive method in the kitchen? Maybe it's someone short on time. Maybe it's someone who can't afford to keep topping up the fresh stuff before it goes bad. Maybe it's someone with mobility issues or chronic pain, or it's a neurodivergent person who struggles with long, multistep tasks. Maybe it's someone who loves fresh garlic but is, for whatever reason, not able to chop it themselves.

Because of this, it's hard to watch a chef's YouTube video or read through a recipe without constantly being reminded that the food I make will never be good enough. Sometimes, it's hard to believe you can be a good cook at all while being disabled.

*

As my condition worsened, I kept pushing myself physically—because who was I if not someone who could pride herself on her food? I kept laughing at jokes about the kind of person who used pre-minced garlic, not wanting to admit that that could be me. And I stopped enjoying spending time in the kitchen, as the pain I felt while I cooked lingered for hours or days afterwards. I avoided cooking as much as possible, often ordering in and eating frozen meals instead.

The more time went on, the more I came to understand disability and casual ableism. As I spoke to other disabled people who used accessibility tools such as electric jar openers or mandolin slicers in their own kitchens, I came to understand that these tools wouldn't make me a bad cook: they would just allow me to enjoy cooking at all. As my symptoms became chronic, I learned to accept that being disabled meant navigating the world a little differently and that reaching for tools to make my life easier wasn't a personal failing.

Eventually, I stocked my kitchen with all the things I simply needed: ground pepper, shredded cheese, a bright yellow bottle of lemon juice. Hesitant to leave fresh garlic behind, I bought pre-peeled cloves before eventually relenting, reaching for a little jar of the pre-minced stuff. And, as cooking became easier, it also became fun again.

There are days when the ableism in cooking still makes me feel alienated. Even as someone who talks openly and often about my struggles with the use of my hands, I face ableism from friends and colleagues who don't know any better. Under a tweet where I simply said, "Pre-minced garlic is good, actually," an acquaintance responded that Anthony Bourdain would be rolling in his grave. (The account has since been deleted.) Another posted a meme about how wrong I was. One person—a stranger—told me this opinion was the reason we should end our species altogether; pre-minced garlic is apparently the grounds for mass extinction.

Though I'd like to say that seeing the suggestion made under a lighthearted tweet didn't bother me, I'm afraid to report it did.

I'm not here to argue that pre-minced garlic tastes the same as the fresh stuff (it doesn't) nor that any of the alternatives I've mentioned are equivalent to their fresh counterparts. I'm here to say the way we talk about accessible food options—whether in our homes, in recipe books, or in cooking shows—needs to change.

The question of why someone might use pre-minced garlic is less important than this one: Does it matter?

Cooking should be about the joy of making something you're excited to eat or serve—about preparing food you like in whatever way works best for you.

You can cook the way you want to. You can even say your way is better, if you like. But there's no reason to say other ways are wrong or disgusting. The simple truth is that being a good cook isn't exclusively about using "high-quality" ingredients. It's about making great food with what's available to you.

In my little kitchen, I toss pre-sliced mushrooms and pre-minced garlic in sizzling oil, filling my apartment with a rich allicin smell. And I feel comfortable in my skills, even if fresh garlic is absent from my pantry.

Hamed Esmaeilion

THE FIGHT OF MY LIFE

I first saw Parisa in the mid-1990s, while she was standing in line to register for dentistry school at Iran's University of Tabriz. I was enrolling in the same program, and I was immediately drawn to her style. The regime of the Islamic Republic, which had swept into power during the 1979 revolution, mandated that all women and girls over the age of nine wear a hijab in public. If they refused, they risked fines, lashings, and imprisonment. Women also had to wear manteaux—long, loose coats that covered everything—and stick to modest colours like black or grey. But Parisa often wore little splashes of red or a cream manteau over jeans. Her glasses were framed in white. It wasn't enough to cause trouble, just enough to signal her feminist beliefs. These choices, by the woman who would later become my wife, were quiet acts of rebellion.

Parisa was with her father, a conservation officer, who, per another regime requirement, was acting as her guardian. Her mother, a teacher, had planned to join them, but the authorities didn't approve of the way she wore her hijab and turned her away. They'd travelled from Sari, a city in northern Iran where

Parisa grew up with her two younger siblings. My own father worked for the national oil refinery company. I grew up in Kermanshah, a city in the west that was one of the centres for Iran's oil industry. We were both eighteen when we started university, both tired of living under a fundamentalist regime.

Under the Islamic Republic, girls could be forced into marriage at thirteen, and they couldn't marry without a male guardian's consent. They couldn't obtain a passport or travel without their husband's permission, and they couldn't seek divorce. Women were banned from being judges and serving in top positions of government. They couldn't appear in public with a single man, unless they were related, without risking consequences. The morality police enforced the rules, and the Islamic Revolutionary Guard Corps, a specialized security and military organization, protected the regime and quashed unrest. Every Iranian knew that the police and the IRGC were always watching.

Over the first four years of university, Parisa and I rarely spoke. Sometimes we would pass each other in the hallways, wearing our white lab coats, but even as classmates, I couldn't call her to talk casually. We would be kicked out of university—or worse—if we were caught. Still, I longed to get to know her. She was serious and studious, always getting top marks. She knew classic and modern literature and never held back her opinions. She advocated for the rights of women, children, and minorities. Parisa saw me as a troublemaker. I was hotheaded and involved in everything except my studies. After the first year, no one expected me to graduate. I skipped school regularly to go to the cinema. I poured my energy into writing, angrily criticizing Iran's politics, but I published under a pseudonym, afraid of what university authorities would do to me if they read my words.

By our fifth and final year of school, I couldn't stop thinking about Parisa—especially her voice, which was soft and sweet. As the men's class representative to the university administration, I was allowed to meet with the women's class representative, who was friends with Parisa. At one of our meetings, I casually mentioned that I liked Parisa. The next time we met, the friend reported back: the feeling was mutual. For several weeks, Parisa's friend acted as a messenger, eventually helping to arrange a phone call.

I didn't own a phone, so one evening I went to a friend's apartment at the appointed time, sat in the hallway, and called Parisa's dormitory. We knew that telephone operators monitored calls, so we had to watch what we said. I pretended I was her brother. We made plans to go for dinner. I had friends who specialized in arranging secret dates, and they told me of a pizza shop where we could meet upstairs without scrutiny. I worried that she wouldn't come; all the courage required for our first date fell solely on her shoulders. As a woman, she took a great risk: she could be detained by police, fined, even arrested. She came anyway.

We stayed for three hours. I ate all the pizza. I would occasionally offer her a bite, and she'd shake her head. I blabbered about books, an audio recording of *The Little Prince*, university. We decided to tell our parents and a few friends about our burgeoning relationship—Parisa didn't want to lie to her family—but agreed to keep it a secret at school. She would call me for ten minutes or so every few days, and that was it. I would reorganize my day at the university to catch a glimpse of her. I'd go to the prosthetics lab to joke around with my friend because I knew she'd be there making plaster moulds for her patients. By summer, I was so deeply in love that I couldn't bear to go a single day without seeing her. I wrote about my love for her in my diaries and gave them to her. I quit smoking because she didn't like it.

At the time, arranged marriages were common in Iran. We wanted to break that tradition, but we still wished for our parents' approval. After one year of dating, I travelled with my parents to visit her family so they could meet and consent to our marriage. Full of nerves about the day, Parisa and I had debated what to do about shoes as my family entered her family's house. Parisa hated when people left their shoes on in someone's home. She thought it unsanitary. We agreed in advance that my family would remove theirs as a sign of respect. She appreciated the gesture, and my parents instantly loved her.

On the way back to university the next day, I was waiting at the bus terminal, elated as I thought about our future, when I heard her voice: "Mr Esmaeilion?" I laughed. She was always so formal. I used to tease her, "When are you going to call me Hamed?" We had one hour together as we waited for our buses. Now that we were engaged, we could walk and sit together without fear. If we got arrested, we could tell the police to call our parents.

Following graduation, I did the standard military service for men, and she did the public service required for women, each lasting two years. During that time, we started planning our wedding. On our invitations, we omitted the typical opening phrase: *In the name of God*. Instead, we chose a stanza from feminist Iranian poet Forough Farrokhzad, whose work had been banned in Iran after the revolution: "If you come to my house, friend, bring me a lamp and a window that I can look through at all the happy people."

We were married in 2003. Afterwards, Parisa suggested that we move to Canada for a better life, free of interference from the republic. But I was a revolutionary in my own way. I was ada-mant. "We have to stay here," I would tell her. "We have to build this country." I wasn't alone. Many young people thought we could help restore democracy. I soon realized that this hope was an illusion. Shortly after our wedding, the conservative support-ers of Iran's new Supreme Leader for life, Ali Khamenei, won a spate of local elections, dashing my dreams.

The next day, Parisa and I went to see an immigration lawyer. It took almost six years for the paperwork to go through. On May 23, 2010, soon after our visas were approved, Parisa gave birth to our daughter, Reera, in Pars Hospital in Tehran. In Mazandarani, the local language in northern Iran, her name means "clever woman." She was born healthy and perfect, all bright eyes and wide grin. We counted down the days until we could leave Iran, knowing that Reera would grow up in a place where she would never be forced to wear a hijab. She would choose whom she wanted to play with and what jobs she wanted to pursue. She would be free from the watchful eyes of the regime. Parisa and I would be too.

*

We arrived in Toronto on December 9, 2010. The blistering cold was a shock, but we were so happy to be free of the Islamic Republic. Parisa never once put on a hijab in Canada. Instead, she wore yellow sweaters and bright sleeveless dresses. We set-tled in Don Valley Village, where there is a large Iranian community. We missed our families back home but never experienced the depression people often have when they immi-grate to a new country. We didn't give ourselves time to. Instead, we jumped right into working toward what we wanted to accomplish. Parisa convinced me that we should take the exam to get certified as dentists in this country. We made a pact: no parties, no shenanigans, just studying. For our first two years in Canada, we read and talked dentistry nonstop in our tiny apartment. One of us would sit at the table studying and the other would play with Reera, then we'd switch.

If Parisa couldn't answer a question while we studied, she would get upset. She'd scour her Farsi and English textbooks to find a solution. And, whenever I grew frustrated, I'd ask her for help. After one year of studying, we took the exam in February 2012. Before we even got the results, Parisa started applying to become a dental assistant and going for job interviews. When we received our marks, six weeks later, she had scored 92 percent. I got 83 and was quite happy with that. The three of us—me, Parisa, and Reera—danced in celebration in our apartment.

Parisa got a job offer in Hanover, a small town of roughly 7,500 residents almost two hundred kilometres northwest of Toronto, so we moved. In time, I started working as a dentist in Elliot Lake. I'd leave Hanover on Monday morning, drive six hours to my clinic, stay in a tiny apartment and return on Friday. At night, I kept writing, always about Iran. I'd published two books before we moved to Canada—short story collections, including one that won a prestigious literary prize in Iran. I wrote a third book, a novel, that was awaiting publication when we immigrated. The Ministry of Culture reviewed every word of a writer's manuscript. They'd remove references to alcohol, to politics, and to women and men spending time together. I still don't know why that third book, which was finally published in 2014, wasn't censored or banned. In it, I included a scene that I'd adapted from a true story told to me by an Iranian colleague. She'd had two brothers, both political activists, who were arrested by the IRGC. After guards tortured and murdered her brothers, they dropped their bodies down the family's outdoor toilet.

Soon after the book came out, Parisa's father had a heart attack. Her brother called us at 3 am and said we must come back. We got on a plane the next day. I was nervous about what would happen to me because of the book, but I didn't say anything to Parisa. She was already in enough anguish. After we landed, a man approached me by name at the airport and asked me to come with him to an office called the passport verification centre—in reality, an IRGC intelligence office. I was allowed to enter the country but had to present myself again later for questioning. They asked why I lived in Canada, and they wanted to know why I had written that scene. After a long day of interrogation, I made it home to Parisa's family at 6 pm. Her father died one hour later.

I spent the entire trip in fear. My wife and daughter were devastated by the loss of their father and grandfather. Meanwhile, I could not be there to support them. I would walk out onto the street and know I was being watched. The IRGC could arrest me anytime and put me in prison for no reason. I wasn't sure I would ever be comfortable in Iran, but I refused to let the regime's scare tactics stop me from writing. As someone living outside the country, I could write aggressively against the regime. I didn't want to give that up. I told Parisa that if I died suddenly, she should go to my publisher and ensure that all my writings would be printed. She memorized the publisher's name. Once, she woke me in the middle of the night to confirm that she recalled it correctly.

In 2017, we bought a house in Richmond Hill and opened a dental clinic together in Aurora. Our parents would come and stay for months at a time to help with Reera. She was a beautiful girl, happy, funny, and stubborn. I used to make her practise the piano for thirty minutes every day, and at nine years old, she came to show me something she'd found on the internet: a statistic that said twenty to twenty-five minutes a day was suitable for piano practice for a kid her age. I laughed and relented. As much as she disliked piano, she loved soccer. She used to play left-back, but just in case she was ever called on to switch roles, we reviewed the skills needed for different positions. Her real sporting triumph was on the monkey bars. She told me that she had beaten everyone in her class, girls and boys, at hanging off the bars during recess. She used to practise at home on a collapsible set we bought her.

Then, in 2019, Parisa's sister, who is a doctor in Iran, called to say that she was getting married. Parisa was ecstatic and began planning her trip back for the wedding. We decided that it was too risky for me to go but that Reera would join her. Parisa bought tickets on a Ukraine International Airlines flight, which would take off from Toronto and then fly to Kyiv for a stopover before continuing on to Tehran.

As their departure grew closer, the situation in Iran intensified. On November 15, 2019, during what would become known as Bloody November, protests over fuel prices broke out around the country. The regime shut down the internet to block its depravity from the world's eyes, but according to Reuters, as many as 1,500 protesters were killed. I asked Parisa not to go. I was scared that something terrible would happen and I wouldn't be there to protect my wife and daughter. Later that night, I apologized. This was a once-in-a-lifetime celebration for her sister and family, and it was important to her. Over the next three weeks, we got Parisa and Reera ready to go. We bought gifts for everyone in Iran. We bought Christmas presents for Reera and wrapped them.

They were flying out on Christmas Day. We let Reera open one gift—a video game—that morning, with the promise that she could open the rest when they returned. She squealed when she opened it. We played for two hours before I drove them to the airport. I watched them walk away from me and through the doors into the passengers-only area. I stood there until Parisa texted me that they were through security.

I didn't know then that this was the last time I would see my wife and daughter alive.

*

The conflict in Iran worsened over the next twelve days. On January 3, a US drone strike killed IRGC major general Qasem Soleimani at Baghdad International Airport. The rising tension between the US and Iran set off alarm bells around the world. I sat up late at night, watching the news, writing and worrying about my family. I wanted to re-book their flights to get them home early, but Parisa told me to stop fretting. She would see me at the airport in Toronto on January 8, as planned.

Finally, the day of their return arrived. Parisa and I spoke briefly when the taxi was on its way to pick them up at her mother's house. I worked that afternoon at my clinic. After finishing with a patient, I glanced at Facebook and saw that Iranian forces had launched ballistic missiles at two locations in Iraq where American personnel were located. I thought about the last war between Iran and Iraq. It started in 1980, when Parisa and I were toddlers. For years, Iraqi jets relentlessly bombed my hometown. There were many days when I did not think we would survive.

The war finally ended in 1988, in part because the US Navy mistook Iran Air Flight 655 for a fighter jet and shot it down. One of my neighbours, a middle-aged man, was among the 290 passengers and crew who were killed. I still remember seeing his memorial notice posted in the streets.

Thinking back to that period, I felt sick. For the first time in my career, I cancelled the rest of my appointments. I kept calling Parisa, but it was no use. Her phone did not have roaming. Eventually, I reached her sister, who said that they had checked in at the airport ten minutes earlier. She calmed me down. I looked at the airline's website and saw that it had a navigation tool to follow planes. I sat in my office and watched Flight PS752 take off on time. I followed the little dot all the way to the border. I felt such relief when it crossed out of Iranian territory.

I didn't realize that the navigation tool was charting the flight path their plane was supposed to take, not the actual plane. That night, in my blissful ignorance, I walked away from my computer. I washed the dishes. I cleaned the floor. I double-checked that Parisa's car was filled with gas for her first day back at work. The only thing I had left to do was buy flowers for them.

Then I looked at my phone. I saw eight missed calls from Iran. That's when I learned the news that destroyed my life. A few minutes after takeoff, Flight PS752 had crashed into the ground and exploded southwest of Tehran with 176 passengers and crew on board. There were no survivors. We have a saying in Farsi: there is no colour after darkness. I never speak about that first hour in the darkness. I've shared much of my story with the world, but that first hour belongs to me.

*

That night, friends found me standing outside of our house, shivering in a T-shirt and shorts. They booked my ticket to Iran immediately. I needed to bury the bodies of my wife and daughter. I needed answers. At Pearson airport, a man in front of me in the security line-up was crying. He was too distraught to organize his belongings to get through the scanner. I asked him whom he had lost, and he said his son and wife. I told him that we should not let them break us. He asked me whom I meant by "them," and I said, "The regime."

As we flew to Frankfurt for our connecting flight, the attendant sat with me and cried. On my next flight, to Tehran, five of the passengers had lost ten people in the downing of PS752. We were flying over Turkey when the pilot announced that we could not land in Tehran for security reasons. American officials had just declared that PS752 had been felled by a missile strike from Iran. We returned to Germany. I didn't arrive in Iran until the next day. Three lawyers I met on my flight told me that they would intervene if I had problems at passport control, but I got through with no trouble. With that, I entered the last building my loved ones had been in before they were murdered.

I fell into the arms of our mothers and Parisa's sister. Already, DNA from Parisa's grandparents had been used to identify her body; my parents' DNA was used to identify Reera's. That night, in my mother-in-law's home, I imagined my wife and daughter packing their suitcases, adjusting items to make room for Reera's new books and dolls. Sometime between their departure from this room and my arrival, their lives had ended and, in effect, so had mine.

That night, under mounting international pressure, the Iranian government released a shameful statement acknowledging that it had shot down the plane. The regime offered no explanation. As details emerged about Iran's culpability, I changed my mind about burying my family in the country and instead insisted on bringing them home to Canada. I demanded to see their bodies. Everyone told me not to, but I needed to bear witness. They were being held in a morgue and had already been placed into coffins, which were wrapped in the flag of the Islamic Republic and piled six high. Writing on them identified the remains. I found one marked "Martyr Parisa Eghbalian." Another, marked "Martyr Reera Esmaeilion," was higher up. My daughter's coffin, I assumed, was lighter than most of the others. The regime was trying to present their deaths as an act of loyalty. Representatives from the Islamic Republic came to my parents' place to install a banner with a congratulatory message about Parisa and Reera being Iranian martyrs. We refused. At a memorial that Parisa's grandfather held for her and Reera, the IRGC hijacked the service and put its representatives behind the podium.

The regime still won't admit the full horror of what it did. We now know that Parisa and Reera's plane was the tenth to fly out of the Tehran airport that morning. It was functioning perfectly. The flight did not deviate from the pre-approved course that I'd followed online. Its takeoff, at 6:12 am, was delayed but otherwise normal. One minute later, the operator of an Iranian surface-to-air missile system categorized the passenger jet as a threat. At 6:14 am, the operator fired a missile at the plane. The pilot appears to have made an effort to turn the plane around. About thirty seconds later, an operator fired a second missile. A fire broke out on board before the plane hit the ground and exploded. Later that afternoon, the Iranian government bulldozed the crash site like it wanted to erase my wife, my daughter, 174 other people, and the plane that had carried them from history.

I fought hard to bring my wife and daughter home. The transport company said that there was no room on my flight. There was a backlog because of the number of flights cancelled in Iran after the crash. I travelled with my parents and Parisa's mother. Our moms were so devastated that they couldn't stand, so we pushed them in wheelchairs. As our flight took off out of Tehran, I counted, the same way I had always counted with Reera, who was afraid of flying: *one, two, three* . . . Three minutes after take-off, I looked out at how high our plane was. This is how high they were when they were shot out of the sky. The next day, Parisa's and Reera's bodies followed me to Canada. They are buried in Elgin Mills Cemetery, under a monument called *Winter* that depicts three broken trees. This is an eternal winter for us. After this February comes another February, then another February.

Two months after the crash, the other families and I formed the Association of Families of Flight PS752 Victims. We wanted to be united in our grief, to keep the memories of our loved ones alive, and to seek justice and answers. I've never been silent about the regime, and now I'm joined by hundreds, supported by thousands. We don't want an apology. We don't want compensation. We want the truth. We want the culprits, the perpetrators and commanders of this atrocious crime, to be identified and brought before the International Criminal Court.

After the crash, the IRGC mixed up the victims' remains and failed to do proper DNA tests. Their belongings were looted. Their luggage, their passports—everything was gone. The only things I got back were a cellphone and the key to our house in Richmond Hill. Eight months later, the RCMP gave me Parisa's

Apple Watch. I can turn it on, but it doesn't give me any information about the three minutes and forty-two seconds that they were in the air. I would like to know everything she did and felt in that time. One day, while I was walking in Toronto, a stranger stopped me on the street. She recognized me from a TV interview and said she had Reera's OHIP card. It had been given to the wrong family. I keep it in my bookshelf, alongside Parisa's dentistry textbooks. I have my wife's OHIP card now, too, also returned to me by a stranger, who messaged me on Instagram.

I cried constantly the first year after their deaths. On Reera's tenth birthday, I wrote her a letter. "I am deeply sorry, my sweet little girl, that the future for you, your mom, and for me turned into cold ashes." After two years, all I wanted to do was die. I kept telling myself that I needed to survive so that people would know the injustice inflicted upon my family and so many others.

So many people complained about being confined to their homes during Covid. Confinement is more tolerable than devastation. Some of my family came to stay with me because life had become unbearable for them in Iran. At night, no one could sleep in our house; you could hear people crying in their rooms. The door to Reera's room remains closed, her wrapped Christmas presents inside. No one goes in there. I see her monkey bars folded in the closet, still waiting for her to return. I've cut my hair short and grown a beard; Parisa did not like it this way. But no one who is alive cares what my hair looks like. I smoke now.

*

In September, I sat at my computer, stunned by the news coming via Facebook from Iran: the morality police had detained twenty-two-year-old Mahsa Amini after deciding that she was wearing her hijab inappropriately, allegedly showing too much of her hair. She fell into a coma while in police custody and died three days later at a hospital in Tehran. Authorities claimed that she had died of heart failure, but no one believes that. This is a murderous regime. Her father says that she had no pre-existing medical conditions. When he finally saw her body, there were bruises on her legs. He believes that she was beaten to death.

Mahsa Amini was around the same age that Parisa—who had always bent the clothing rules—was when we got engaged. What happened to Amini resonated with me and with people everywhere. It added new heat to long-simmering anger. It's like we lost our loved ones again. Iran has erupted in protests. People are fed up with the violence. They are tired of suffering. They are tired of murder, incompetence, and fear. They are tired of women being denied an experience as basic as feeling the wind rushing through their hair. They are so angry that they are willing to risk their lives. They want to be free.

Like many, I worry about the risk of violence in Iran. That's why I continue to protest. We're fighting against our country's injustice and calling for change, for democracy. We're keeping the world's eyes on Iran. Since Amini's death, my team and I have organized protests in Toronto, Vancouver, Montreal, Ottawa, and other cities across Canada. I spoke at a United Nations protest in New York. I worked with a team of activists to put together a rally in Berlin, where 100,000 people showed up. My phone goes off every minute, a hundred messages an hour from people in Iran, families in the association, reporters.

This is a revolution. Everybody knows that. It is not unrest. I cannot let my grief isolate me. I must show up for myself, for the other families and for the Iranian people. We want the Canadian government to ban high-ranking members of the IRGC from Canada and to increase sanctions against powerful, wealthy Iranians—similar to the sanctions we've seen recently against Russian oligarchs. We want an investigation by the International Civil Aviation Organization into Flight PS752. We want the IRGC declared a terrorist organization.

Some people have told me that I am going too far, that I should stay out of a fight with the regime, that this fight will destroy me. But it is too late for that. I have lost everything. I live in the darkness. Like many others in the Iranian diaspora, I try to echo the voices of the voiceless. Recently, I watched a video of a teenager in Sari, Parisa's hometown. She ripped off her headscarf, danced with it and then tossed the garment into a fire. I knew that this is what Parisa would have wanted to see: Iranians fighting for their freedom. And, in that moment, my heart broke all over again.

Kate Gies

///////////

FOREIGN BODIES

*Note: This piece makes reference to body trauma
and contains a mention of child abuse.*

My friends on Ward 7C are, like me, the kids under construction.
Cut to fit the shapes of other kids, but never quite fitting.

*

Julia is three. Her hair is shaved, and a big scar stretches from ear
to ear across to the top of her head, like a worm fat with rain. She
was born with her eyes drooped into her cheeks and the doctors
cracked her skull open to set things right. So she could see like
other kids see. She's too sick to leave her bed, but sometimes she
clutches its metal bars and pulls herself up. Sometimes she sings
"The Wheels on the Bus" in a squeaky little voice and we come
to her room and sing and clap along. She giggles and her eyes
roll around like lost marbles, searching for our faces. When we
get loud, the nurse comes in. She tells us Julia needs to rest. She

pulls Julia's hands from the metal bars and settles her into the bed. Julia tries to close her eyes and they turn into slippery white balls. Her eyelids don't work yet.

*

Every time I come back for another operation, the smell of 7C smacks me in the face—bleach, old milk, the rotting orange that each of us brings back from the operating room. Barf. The smells all mix together into a soup that flows through the hallway. After a day or two, the smell seeps into my skin and I become part of the soup.

*

In the lobby of the hospital, there are two big displays of "Foreign Bodies" that kids have swallowed or jammed inside themselves. Rotting peanuts, coins the size of Ping-Pong balls, Monopoly pieces, buttons, long rusty nails, and, most creepy, open safety pins, some as big as a Swiss Army knife. On 7C, we talk a lot about these displays. It's one of the first things we ask each other when we meet. "Have you seen the displays of Foreign Bodies?" I don't know what gets us most, the fact that kids freely chose to stuff these things inside themselves, or the fact that the things they stuffed inside themselves didn't kill them. We ask each other which of the objects we would choose to have stuck inside us if we had to have one stuck inside us. Most of us say the small buttons or the little dog from the Monopoly set. Some of us, when we need to feel brave, will say the nails or the big open safety pin.

*

Tim shows me the thin scar between his thumb and pointing

finger as we wait for our pre-op photos outside the photography room. He tells me he once had an extra thumb there. Two thumbs on one hand! I want to ask if he's mad they cut it off. Couldn't an extra thumb come in handy? Instead, I ask if he misses it. He tilts his head, says "sometimes." His dad has signed him up for baseball this summer because he can now fit his hand inside a baseball glove. "I'm going to be the next Kelly Gruber," he says. He doesn't sound excited. He tells me he can still feel it, the cut-off thumb. Like it's a miniature ghost haunting his hand.

*

There are rules in the photography room. Those of us who've been there before know the rules well and make sure to prepare the first-timers before they go in. The pointy-faced photographer pretends to be a fun guy but gets mad when we don't do things the way he wants. In the photography room, we sit on a stool and have to keep our lips relaxed (these aren't the kind of pictures we're supposed to smile in). The photographer bends and twists us in ways we're not used to, and we have to stay very still in whatever shape he puts us into. After he fiddles with his camera, he says "Boom!" clicks a button, and the umbrellas behind him explode with light. It's very important not to flinch.

*

Before our operations, we have to put on mint-green hospital gowns because they open right up and the surgeons don't have to fuss around to get to our bodies. All of the hospital gowns have "The Property of the Hospital for Sick Children" stamped on the bottom in a little triangle. Like anyone would ever steal a hospital gown! None of us like wearing them because they leave us bare-naked at the back, and once we put it on, we know it isn't coming off for at least a couple of days after our operations. We also don't like wearing them because once we slip our arms through the mint-green sleeves, we, too, become The Property of the Hospital for Sick Children.

*

Erica teaches me how to open the large steel door on the ward fridge so we can swipe Popsicles when the nurses aren't looking. We creep into the hall, our slippers soft on the speckled floor. We look right, we look left, and when it's clear, we wrap our hands around the fridge handle and pull hard. The purple birthmark splotched on Erica's face crimps as the door swings open. The cold air blows over us like the breath of an ice witch. We run from the fridge, Popsicles numbing our hands, and her blond ringlets bounce like Slinkys. After my operation, I'm too dizzy to move much, so Erica slips into my room with a cherry Popsicle (my favourite!). I slurp it down faster than I should. It's still cold when I barf it up a few seconds later.

*

There's a computer on wheels near the nurses' station, and when we're bored, some of us kids drag it into one of our rooms and plug it in. It only plays *Frogger*. In the game, we're frogs who have to cross a busy street and a crocodile-filled river to get home safely. Most of us don't make it.

*

I meet Becky in the playroom on the sixth floor. She shows me her half-eaten apple, says she ate the half in one big bite. I don't believe her, but I nod anyway. She has black hair and pink cheeks and one of her arms is snaked with jagged red skin. "It died," she says about her arm and dimples stamp into her pink cheeks. I ask her who killed it and she tells me it's a mystery. I find out later that her dad did it, poured hot coffee on her when she took too long to eat her Cheerios. He isn't allowed in the hospital.

*

I first see Laura on my way back from the bathroom. I recognize myself in her instantly. Our backs are bent by the same big cuts the surgeons made on our bellies and our chests and our necks. Our backs pull us down, like we're trying to say sorry. When the nurse tells me there's another girl on the ward born without a right ear, I tell her I already know. Laura and I don't talk about operations or ears. Instead, we cram ourselves into the movie booth in the playroom and watch half-hour cartoons for a quarter. There's room for just the two of us and our thighs touch and our knees knock together. It doesn't matter that the cartoons are corny and babyish. It's enough to be in the booth together. It's enough to know someone else like us exists.

*

When the pack of surgeons come to the ward, we all get very quiet and hurry to our rooms to wait to be look at. There's a different smell when the surgeons come—sweat mixed with cologne. Sometimes, a surgeon presses his hands into a sore spot and a scream cracks open in one of us. The scream gallops all the way down the hall. When it reaches each of us in our rooms, lying on our crinkly bedsheets, we hold the places we've been sliced into, our cuts humming like mouths clamped shut.

David Huebert

FLESH MADE BURN

A Vasectomy Revenant

N is working, so it's my mother who picks me up. In the months leading up to the vasectomy, I'd gotten the sense that my mother opposed the operation—I'd thought she wanted more grand-kids, or thought it was too soon to make such a final choice. Here, in the car, on the street we've driven a thousand times, she tells me about my father, how he refused this same procedure. We talk about sex, speak with unusual frankness. She tells me about women who, after having children, make their husbands wear condoms for the rest of their sexual lives, how she couldn't stand that. I chuckle nervously, then feel ashamed for construct-ing this barrier. It does not deter. She tells me about this zone, this part of my body. "I think you have some childhood trauma there."

*

On the morning of the operation, shave the hair from the front surface of the scrotum using an ordinary razor, such as a Trac II.

You should wear snug-fitting underwear, such as briefs, not boxers, and you should arrange for a drive home.

*

I lie bare-loined in a hoodie, sock feet crinkling on crepe paper. The doctor is bland and blond and affable. He is middle-aged, middle-height, middle-build, perfect toothed, white as Red Mill, as me. This morning I shaved my scrotum for the first time, thought of it as a "scrotum" for the first time. The doctor asks me to uncross my ankles, begins to scrub with sterile pads, readies the syringe. The surgical light descends, a humming UFO. I glance at the analogue clock, the popcorn ceiling, my mind all needle. The pain is thin and distant, fierce and dull.

There is a scalpel, a small pair of tweezers. A drum-machine, a tambourine, a synthesizer. Two little sutures, he told me. They'll dissolve on their own. Not even a stitch. There is a clamp he pins onto the flesh and uses to keep the wound open as he works. There is frequent suction. There is not enough scenery, so I tense into the music—a voice full of islands and desire. The music feels off, too cheerful. But what is the right soundtrack for minor, elective torture?

The cauterizer comes into view, a gleaming, pencil-thin serpent. I clench and breathe as the smoke wisps up in reeking curlicues. Smoke that had been my body and the room ripe with it: the smell of flesh made burn.

*

A vasectomy is a permanent form of contraception and although it can be reversed in certain cases, this cannot be relied upon. You must be confident that your family is complete.

*

In the weeks leading to the operation, that last line becomes a hauntology of my bourgeois self. Born in the violent shock wave of settler privilege, I never believed and always knew I'd have such a normal, perfect, healthy, white family.

What does it mean for a family to be "complete"? Before the knife, in this moment of powerful and self-subscribed medicalized vulnerability, I feel myself as a parodic castration anxiety meme.

For weeks, I feed on dilemma—is my family complete? Some macabre hypotheticals I entertain: the high expense of a reverse vasectomy, which is not guaranteed to succeed; the cousin of a friend, who got a "commitment vasectomy" because his wife was unable to bear children and thought this would bind them in sterility; the rare case where the vas deferens regrows in a reptilian phantasm of cellular regeneration.

But here is the crux of the crisis: My spouse, N, is certain she does not want more kids. I'm sure I want to continue my marriage to her for as long as she'll let me. On the one hand I will want N's sympathy, on the other hand she will rightly remind me that what I have just gone through is a footnote on the suffering of lifelong birth control, not to mention giving birth. The surgery is a choice I've made. But I am also an ambivalent person, a writer and teacher who trades in nuance. I am trained to look at the other side of problems, to indulge FOMO, court what-ifs.

Consider my two human aporias, two curly-headed cherubs, two giggling, scampering synecdoches of manhood and mirth. The astonishment that such beings could be made from nothing, called from the void. My eldest, R, re-rigging the lyrics of "Mr Mistoffelees" to suit our fluffy white cat, Moby-Dick. My youngest, S, asking if today is her "happy birthday." R saying she can't wait to become a woman so her vagina will bleed like her mother's. The four of us laughing, cackling. The four of us listening to Dan Mangan while the children pretend the bath is a pool. Kick kick kick. The four of us. How could this be complete when all I want is the mush of now and the tumble of tomorrow, a bath time that never ends?

Before having kids of my own, I'd wondered if love was quantifiable, a limited resource. If I loved a new friend, for example, would I love my parents less? What I have realized in four short years as a parent is that children breed love. Making children reveals that love is exponential—the more you make, the more love fills your world. To make tiny humans, then, is to populate the world with love. Yes, this is politically problematic. Yes, there are mouths to feed, there is a hungering, overfull world. No, love cannot be the only factor. Still—this blooming, exponential, expanding universe of love—isn't it pretty to think with?

*

Vasectomy is an operation in which the sperm-carrying tubes are cut and clipped to prevent sperm from entering the semen. There are two tubes, one on each side, called the vas deferens, which carry sperm from the testicle.

*

I am five years old in the slant-ceilinged upstairs of the house on Duncan Street. It is the moment of gleeful nudity after bath time, but my father has a burrowing look, a wiggle in his moustache. Come here, he says, kneeling, indicating my genitals. I trust him absolutely, yet I hesitate, stand naked in the stark intimacy of

Being Examined. Maybe there are motes of dust in the late afternoon. Maybe it's winter, the house bright with eighties bulbs. My father calls my mother's name in his should-we-be-worried voice. My mother appears, kneels, inspects my testicles. I listen, parse. An imbalance. One of them should be lower than it is. "It's okay," my father tells me. "It's all right," he says. "You'll be fine." His eyes are certain as doubt.

*

Remember that you are NOT STERILE IMMEDIATELY after the operation.

*

The term "vas deferens" derives from the Latin for "vessel" and "carrying forth." To close it off is to sever a possibility. Yes, this possibility is far from innocent, drenched in reproductive normativity. Still, the choice to sterilize myself is the most symbolically significant body modification I'll ever undergo. The testicles are the most richly (and problematically) textured symbolic zone in the male body. They mean health. They mean chest-beating virility. They hang, dangling and metallic, from the trailer hitches of my memory. They contain, as queer theorist Lee Edelman has rightly criticized, a fantasized future.

When I read my doctor's demand for familial closure, I think of what Billy-Ray Belcourt calls "the fantasy of self-sovereignty." Don't the doctors know that no self or family will ever be complete? And isn't it for precisely this reason that I am here, under the knife? To render my desire the melting rainbow road to forever it has always been. I am here to renounce endings, to renounce completion, to sever sex of its pesky biological telos.

Am I living the ultimate repronormativity or amputating the futurity Edelman named the "cult of the child"?

I whisper to the doctor: *This wound is a purgatory, a membrane between completion and prevention.* Am I surprised when he does not hear?

*

The operation is done under local anaesthetic. I use a tiny puncture in the front of the scrotum, through which both the right and the left vas can be cut.

*

I don't remember the operation I had when I was five years old, a standard procedure for an undescended testicle. I don't remember going under. I don't remember vomiting on the floor (an allergy to the opiate Demerol). I remember the plastic helicopter my mother bought me in the hospital store. I know that, thirty years later, when I met my family doctor and told him about it, he said: "So you must have one shriveled testicle?"

*

The vas deferens is an epithelial lined structure like the urethra, bladder, and fallopian tubes, and the regenerative qualities of these structures are well known. Because our bodies are makings, poeses, the vas deferens can regenerate. When I read this, I remember being fascinated, as a boy, by the resilience of an earthworm's body. Though I was too squeamish to hook a worm when fishing, I thrilled in the knowledge that, when cut in two, a worm goes on living. Researching this essay, I will learn this is only, sadly, half true. That earthworms have heads and tails and if the worm is cut carefully and neatly beneath its reproductive area (the clitellum), the head-bit will go on living while the lower half dies.

In the schadenfreude fantasia of Dante's *Divine Comedy*, punishment and crime become coterminous in the principle of contrapasso. Purgatory is Dante's most cunning and most medieval invention. Here the Envious traverse their terrace with their eyes sewn shut. One wonders how Dante might punish those who choose self-sterilization. In *Purgatorio*, Dante provides a memorable metaphor: "do you not know that we are worms and born / to form the angelic butterfly" (10.124–125). Like all Dante's metaphors, this one despises the body and advocates ethereal transformation, the soul's upload to Heaven. Rereading the Italian poet as I prepare for my vasectomy, I want to insist that the butterfly is not superior to the worm, that the worm nourishes the earth, makes life from rot, that the worm should be celebrated not for its potential to transform but for its very worminess, its vermiculate, sinuous self.

The Ancient Greek "crisis" contains the sense of the modern English "decision." Large decisions in life—to have children, to stop having them—are always a kind of crisis. For me, the psychic condition of getting a vasectomy was not unlike that of anticipating having a child. You stand at the edge of a cliff. Who knows quite where the rocks are? You ponder, fret, hesitate. You feel better once you jump.

*

After surgery, I would advise you to go home and put an ice pack on the scrotum (a bag of frozen vegetables from the freezer is an inexpensive and effective ice pack).

*

The doctor tells me to get up slow. To turn my legs around first, then lie back down if I feel light-headed. A ludicrous thought occurs: I feel the same, I feel like me, there's been no fundamental realignment. I think down to the wound in my loins, a metonym for the damaged daily pretense it is to be being a man.

My mother picks me up. We drive by the church and the former Oxford Theatre, and my mother tells me about the myth that children are a decision. The Oxford Theatre is a climbing gym now. My mother tells me that people say they decided to have a kid or didn't and that maybe that's true but it's also true that once you've tumbled off that cliff children decide you, make you, teach you. We exist in relation.

I have been self-sterilized, but it doesn't feel like loss. It feels like change, some alchemy of pleasure and self-control.

Later, N and I will pick up our daughters from daycare. We will take them home, make hot chocolate, negotiate marshmallow colour and quantity. We will blow raspberries, clench hysterical. We will go into our garden, move aside the big rocks, watch the squirming fascination of the worms. We will listen to "Mr Mistoffelees." They will compete for turns of scampering up onto my shoulders, tumble giggling down. They will spin and flail, will be curious about my wound. "Papa bobo?"

As we pull up to my home, I think about fatherhood and self-identity, of being a dad and a man, all those linked fragilities. I think of having issues, having issued. I think of Jake Barnes, the protagonist of Ernest Hemingway's *The Sun Also Rises*. Jake Barnes who received a genital wound in World War I and retreated into sexless melancholy. More fortunate than Jake, I will continue to have (a) sex. But what I have learned from

Hemingway's panicked chest-thumping is that masculinity has always been a scarred and trembling thing, a bloodied and cowering mirror. What I have learned is to try to wear my privilege as my wounds: proud and open, tender and slashed. And in the journey of my learning I have children to sing and dance with, to take to gymnastics class. Children who will prod their father's penis, mimic his pee-stance. Children who will go on making me. And I know, in this analgesic rush, what I could not have told the doctor: that the joy of family is a wound in the thigh of completion, and that I hope it will grow, swell, flourish, and remain as dazzling and livid as any severed worm.

ENDNOTES

Italicized lines are from a handout entitled "Advice to Patients Having a Vasectomy" by Dr Glenn Andrea, MD.
I have quoted Allen Mandelbaum's translation of Dante's *Divine Comedy*.

Jenny Hwang

―――

SILKWORMS

"Among all the creatures of this earth, your name is silkworm.
When flowers blossom and leaves green, you visit me.
We recognize each other like old friends."
―"Meditations on a Silkworm,"
Nam, Hoo Kyung (1912–1978)

It is spring and the pandemic has just begun. My father sits at the
kitchen table as my children run around us. I have recently taken
a step back from work in attempt to bring some order to the
chaos that has ensued with three young children under the age
of eight, now completely sequestered at home. The shutting
down of outside life has strangely also shut down the part of me
that is always running. Always frenetic. The forced cloistering
opening up a spaciousness in me that I have missed. A moment
to ponder possibility over survival. I am feeling slightly embold-
ened and shyly mutter to my father that I might try writing.
"Your grandmother was a good writer," he says, as he uses his

right index finger to scribble into his left palm, miming the motion of pen to paper.

My father has said this to me before; that my grandmother was a good writer. I remember him saying it once in my early teens as I watched him organize our family den. "Your grandmother was a good writer," he said with a quiet pride, as he ruffled through papers filled with Korean words and pulled out the family Jokbo, a book that listed our genealogy tables. I didn't ask for more information back then. This is how most of our communication went. Factual statements. Instructions given. Matters of the day reported. Short fleeing sentences to ensure the efficient transmission of only the most necessary information across our achingly wide lingual and cultural separation.

"Where is my name?" I asked, as my father looked through the Jokbo. "It's here. But when you're married, it will be erased." My younger brother laughed maniacally. "You get erased! Aaahahaha." I protested in feigned dismay, but only for a few seconds, preferring to join in the rare moment of cheerful humour. Who cared if it was at my expense? It never felt productive to be angry about things I could not change. Besides, I was a teenager growing up in Canada. There was no personal consequence for me whether I was in a Jokbo or not, I thought. I did not understand then, how much erasure was happening in real time. Had already happened. The isolation of living in diaspora. The vanishing that happened with assimilation. History never discussed. I didn't think twice about the fact that this was the only piece of information I had ever received about my grandmother. After all, it was my normal; living every day of my existence within the outlines of these shadows. I was not oblivious. I was a realist. Fighting gender beliefs within the family was the least of my concerns.

Our necessity of communicating in the shortest simplest phrases instilled the habit of interpreting my parents' words personally, into what made the most sense to me at any given moment. Sometimes, "Your grandmother was a good writer" meant she had beautiful penmanship, as I imagined her sitting on an ondol floor practising brushstrokes with an ink brush in hand. Other times, I've imagined her writing lovely letters to loved ones overseas. A woman with a knack for words. Like the way my mother asked my father to write the cards when we attended special occasions. Like the way I could write a well-worded email to a friend.

But today in the kitchen, I decide to ask my father what he means exactly.

"She wrote," he says.

"Wrote what?" I ask.

"She just wrote. She was a good writer," he says, I think I see a flicker of annoyance for being asked to clarify.

A few days later my father places a pile of paper into my hands. "Here," he says. Ah. This is what he means. Has meant. My grandmother was a good writer. Here. My Korean is limited and my grandmother wrote in an older vernacular. I am like a preschooler trying to read the King James Bible.

Summer and fall pass quickly. It is winter now. Nearing a year into the pandemic. My grandmother's papers seem to have only moved from my father's drawers to mine during the last several months. My fragmented mind occasionally feeling guilty for their untouched state. The days have shortened and it is cold. The kids have more energy than the bones of our house can hold and I am beginning to feel the cracks. But I have started to write more when I can find the time—a deep source of consolation that keeps me going. I start to look for someone who can decipher my grandmother's words and finally find a wonderful translator on Upwork.

One night a document lands in my inbox. The atmosphere around me thickens and blurs. It is only me and my grandmother's words that are clear. As I read, it is like she is speaking to me through a loop in time. Her voice as real and loud as my children in the next room. *Remember me*, she says. *Hear my story.* Her voice is not stern and stoic like I have always thought it might be. It is soft and warm. It is pleading.

The first of my grandmother's writing to come back to me is titled "Meditations on a Silkworm." I read through it and come to realize that at one point in her life my grandmother was involved in sericulture—the practice of cultivating silkworms for the production of silk. First introduced to Korea in 200 BC, silk once played a vital role in Korean society as an important commodity in economic trade and prized for its beauty and strength. During the Choson Dynasty (1392–1910), a yearly sericultural rite was held, where the queen would demonstrate the rearing of silkworms and make ritual clothes to promote silk growing and weaving.

As I read her piece, it feels like I am learning to breathe for the first time. All the emotion and openness I have thirsted for sitting before me in her words. This is as much a lamentation as it is a meditation. I hear her trying to make peace with suffering and loss, with her disappointments and her questions.

The lifecycle of the silkworm has four stages: egg, larva, cocoon, and adult silk moth. In places where seasons change, the cycle starts in spring, when the silk moth lays its eggs. Ten days later the eggs hatch and tiny silkworms emerge. The silkworms grow and moult several times as they feed on mulberry leaves before entering the next stage. This is where the magic happens. Where the silkworms spin themselves into silk cocoons with a strong single thread that can measure up to a mile long. It is this thread when wound with thread from other cocoons that becomes the precious silk fibre that has been cherished and venerated for thousands of years.

My grandmother describes how year after year in spring, the silkworm comes to visit her—how they recognize each other like old friends. She writes about providing meals to the silkworm and cleaning its waste. Of protecting it through the cold nights and warm days and keeping it safe from predators. She describes how the silkworm soon settles down to cover its entire body with thread, and dangles like a flower as white as winter snow.

She describes the silkworm as a creature to be emulated. A creature who gives and gives and gives, sacrificing everything for humans and gaining nothing in return. A creature who clothes kings and queens in fine garments, and whose body is used to nourish poor men and children. "Your talents are unmatched by any creature of this world," she writes. "But tell me what sins have you committed in your past life. To sacrifice everything for us and gain nothing in return." In traditional sericulture, silkworm cocoons are boiled while the larvae inside are still alive so that the silk threads can be harvested without being broken. I sense the ambivalence she feels with this practice in her writing. And I also note the ambivalence she feels with her own situation, feeling forgotten by her children and grappling with old age.

Unearthing of grief or sadness was something to be feared and avoided in our house—a Pandora's box that should never be opened. Most likely the inaccessibility was very real—the untampered need to keep going at all costs. Through death of loved ones overseas, store robberies, and family illness, it was stoicism and silence that kept everyone safe and kept us moving forward. Expressing sadness while we were treading water would have been ludicrous.

And now here it all is, sadness personified. My grandmother cries her sorrows out onto paper, transforms her tears to words, and sends them down two generations to give me strength. So that I know that I am not the only one who grieves what is wrong and what is hard, and that it is OK to feel.

I know now that my grandmother was left a single mother to four children during the Korean War. Her husband and eldest son separated from her forever once the borders between North and South Korea were made permanent. "What is there to boast of in these developed societies that have been poisoned with greed. Societies still dictated by the law of the jungle, where the strong prey on the weak. A silkworm leaves its silk and body, but a human leaves nothing. I will not overlook the truth I have found in this tiny creature—this generous being." She writes with sadness but also solace. She finds comfort in her silkworm friend whose life she sees as even more self-sacrificing than hers has had to be. And with that she takes courage, and arrives at acceptance.

I think of all the struggles my grandmother must have faced against the life I am situated in now. I think of the independence and freedom that women have, and how isolating and relentless it has all become. How do I continue forward, standing on my grandmother's shoulders? If my grandmother's work was acceptance, can I dare to move toward something more? It's hard to imagine what that looks like; these difficult early years of child-rearing exacerbated by the pandemic.

Early in 2021, the *New York Times* came out with a series on the current crisis of American mothers and titled it "The Primal Scream." They opened up a hotline that would record one-minute calls from mothers sharing their experiences. The recordings were stark; women screaming at the top of their lungs, crying in despair, and venting their rage. It was deeply resonant with my own experience; with the times I had run into my car to scream myself, beating the steering wheel until the palms of my hands were red and raw. Screaming at the impossibility of it. The demands of the world, of children, of family, and my complete inability to meet it all.

I wonder if we had infinitesimal hearing, if this is how the silkworms sound, as they are being boiled alive. Or if they have forgotten to scream at all. Sericulture over thousands and thousands of years have so completely domesticated silkworms that the larvae have lost all of their pigment, and the adult silk moths can no longer fly.

We are midway through the second summer of the pandemic when we find the caterpillars outside. We bring them home and house them in a giant cardboard box, daily replenishing the milkweed with fresh leaves my mother-in-law brings to us from her daily walks. I watch with anticipation as they grow plump and long. Waiting for the signs when they stop feeding and start climbing the sides of the box to look for a safe place to pupate. They are slow enough in their ascent, and I, obsessive enough in my fascination that I can catch them on their journey. I move them to a smaller habitat I can place on a table so I can watch them transform. There are a few that have already escaped me— the wanderers that have decided to go less conventional routes; hiding in the underside of a leaf or the hollow of the half an egg carton I have thrown in for their entertainment. I find them whenever I clean the box—fully formed chrysalis amidst the ruffage like hidden jewels.

I am beyond burned out. I am numb, with three young children hollering and wailing for so many things I no longer have the capacity to give. There is every kind of rage, inadequacy and awfulness stirring inside of me. But outside, life has started opening up. Gatherings and appointments. People. All of a sudden, so many people. The receptionist at the dentist office, neighbours on their walks, friends at outdoor picnics—all greeting me with bright eager faces. "Aren't you enjoying this beautiful weather?" they cheerfully ask. The audacity. I want to shout "No!" but I can't. I am a mother after all.

Thank God for these creatures. Several times a day, I sit and watch them. The kids, the pressures and demands, fading away. The caterpillars are getting ready to pupate now. Spinning silk to latch themselves on to the ceiling of their habitat and slowly bringing themselves to hang head-down. And when they finally begin to settle and completely still, my mind follows. Reminding me that there is breath still inside of me, and that is enough.

It is almost fall. The monarch butterflies are near the end of their metamorphosis. The shiny green cocoons have vanished into a clear veneer, revealing their fiery orange and black spotted wings encased inside. When they hatch, we watch them take a moment to straighten out their wings and say goodbye as they flutter away in search of nearby milkweed.

A few days later we make our way to the Sandbanks beaches in Prince Edward County—a few hours east of the city. Our last hurrah before school will open up for in-person learning in a few weeks. The beach is beautiful. The water is cool and clear, and the sand is soft and smooth. Today I feel hopeful. Like I might be able to partake in the beauty with those around me. As I sit on the sand and look out at the shimmering lake, I am amazed to see several monarch butterflies fluttering along the shoreline. I learn later that monarch butterflies travel along the Great Lakes shorelines as they migrate south for the winter. But on this day, I see delight. My friends. Lifting and landing. Lifting and landing along the sand, for the pleasure of everyone who sees them. It looks like they are dancing.

Fiona Tinwei Lam

———

BAD DAYS

"Coronavirus: Il a rendu plus de gens racistes que malades"
("Coronavirus: it has made more people racist than sick")
—message on a wall in Nantes, France;
Estelle Ruiz photograph in Yasmeen Surhan and Timothy
McLaughlin, "The Other Problematic Outbreak,"
The Atlantic, March 13, 2020

"[W]hite Canadians are the least likely to believe racist attacks
or harassment regularly occur in their neighbourhood or are
happening more often since the pandemic began."
—Ryan Flanagan, "StatCan Survey Shows New Evidence of
Increase in Anti-Asian Sentiment, Attacks,"
CTV News, July 8, 2020

You've tried to write about racism during the pandemic, but the words stutter out onto the page. That long submerged sense of unease bobs to the surface—dread, terror, hurt of course, too, but also an impotent, seething rage. You stop typing. Your hands retreat from the keyboard. You stare out above the screen to the window, not seeing the maples on the boulevard with their shimmering green leaves against the summer sky. The fluttering of the leaves almost mirrors the fluttering in your gut, except there's a sliver of dissonance akin to nausea. The present dredges up the past. What you didn't say. What you didn't do. What was contained out of politeness and a wish not to offend. The import of the words or actions you tried to shrug off, believing it would dissolve.

In the unspoken hierarchy of racisms, you aren't even on the bottom rung—you don't even qualify. Over two centuries of Chinese Canadian history in Canada disappears. The Chinese artisans who settled here in 1788, the gold prospectors in 1858, the fifteen thousand railroad workers who came in the late 1800s. Decades of segregated workplaces and swimming pools and theatres, restrictive covenants on land, race riots, immigration exclusion for two decades, the bars against entering the professions of law, pharmacy, and accountancy. Disenfranchisement.

You're considered part of the problem, perceived as affiliated with a monolithic totalitarian regime you have always condemned and disavowed for its horrific human rights abuses against minorities and activists. You've internalized the dismissal, the skepticism: *That didn't happen. Are you sure? There must be another explanation. That's nothing. Others have it worse. Get over it.* You footnote your truths; otherwise they'll be labelled counterfeit or mere mirage.

It doesn't matter who you actually are: whether you're a recent immigrant or were born here, whether you've lived here one week or half a century, whether you have a Canadian accent or a foreign one, whether you speak English fluently or not at all. It doesn't matter that you've never been to Wuhan, never heard of pangolins until the start of the pandemic, know no one who eats bats, and believe markets in live sea creatures and animals should be banned in the same way massive factory farms and puppy mills and suspect marine parks should be outlawed. Your facial features, your skin colour, your body build all signify "Outsider."

The model minority myth has splintered into tinder. The present equation is simple: all Asians are Chinese; all Chinese embody the virus; you are the virus. You—and anyone who looks vaguely like you—represent a swarm, a teeming masked horde. You are a threat. You are to blame for layoffs, lockdowns, shutdowns, evictions, poverty, illness, death.

At the start of the pandemic, the young blond clerk with a goatee at the local bakery in your neighbourhood radiates hostility when you approach. Scowling, he refuses to give you eye contact. You try a smile. It doesn't work. He takes your order, makes your coffee, and leaves it on the counter, without a word. You hesitantly take the cup, unsure if it's your order, but no one else seems to be waiting. As you sip your drink, you watch him politely engaging with the white customers who arrive after you.

At the restaurant patio, middle-aged men who are conversing in Italian at the table across from you rise to leave. One of them stands for a moment and glares at you, as if on the verge of saying something. You glance at him with a raised eyebrow but continue conversing with your spouse in front of you who is oblivious to his role as your white male shield. You brace yourself to stand and respond if the man dares to utter what seems to be coalescing on his face. He leaves.

At the grocery store, a white customer paying the cashier spots you in the queue ten feet away. He quickly pulls up his mask. At the homeopath's office, a white woman with wavy, shoulder-length grey hair opens the door and sees you seated in the chair. She abruptly stops mid-step. You look up. Your eyes meet. The woman balks at crossing the threshold. "I'm just nervous," she says as another patient arrives behind her, wanting to pass. The other patient squeezes past her into the waiting room. The door closes. Five minutes later, she sidles in to talk to the receptionist, giving you a wide berth.

A white man shouts "Where's your mask?" as you cycle up a hill long before masking becomes mandatory.

These are minor compared to what you hear on the news. In your hometown of Vancouver, you hear reports of Asian Canadians, the majority of them women, being spat at or punched on transit or on the streets. The windows of the Chinese Cultural Centre are defaced with racist graffiti, as are the lions of the Millennium Gate at the entrance to Chinatown.

You watch in disbelief at video footage of a young white man who verbally and physically attacks Patricia Medrano, a married Filipina who has just rejected his repeated attempts to get her phone number. In an Edmonton apartment complex, he lunges at her, kicks a door into her, threatens to decapitate her, shouting profanities and racial slurs about the virus and Wuhan. He even does a "Heil Hitler" salute.[1] It's eerily reminiscent of writer Jiayang Fan's description in the *New Yorker* about being accosted by a leering man who made a sexual gesture, licking his lips while gesturing at her chest, and shouted out "ching chong kung flu." She describes "the split second in which a smidgen of sexual interest transmutes into racist scorn."[2]

At her local grocery store in Edmonton, Abigail Douglass, a Russian-born Chinese Canadian who was adopted and raised by a white family, experiences five racist incidents during a twenty minute shopping trip. In the province of Quebec, a visiting Korean research fellow is stabbed from behind in the neck with a hunting knife. He is in hospital for three days, undergoing surgery and blood transfusions. Pedestrian Huiping Ding, and cyclist Gérard Chong Soon Yuen, both Chinese Canadian, are mowed down separately by a white driver who deliberately turns off his headlights in Brossard. Both victims die of their injuries. Despite the Chinese community's insistence that the issue be investigated further, the local police summarily assert that the driver is not motivated by racism.[3] The lion statues at Montreal's Quan Am Buddhist temple are smashed with a sledgehammer, and then smashed again after their repair.

In the US, Bawi Cung, a Burmese father, and his two young sons who are mistaken for Chinese and blamed for the virus are stabbed while grocery shopping in Midland, Texas. In San Francisco, Vicha Ratanapakdee, an eighty-four-year-old immigrant from Thailand who is taking his usual hour-long walk, is suddenly shoved violently to the ground and dies from a brain hemorrhage. Ninety-four-year-old Anh Peng Taylor, a forty-year resident of the city, is stabbed in the wrist and torso also while taking her usual morning walk. Two Asian women, ages eighty-four and sixty-three are stabbed multiple times while awaiting a bus in San Francisco. In New York, Noel Quintana, a Filipino-born employee at a non-profit working with the mentally disabled, is slashed from ear to ear with a box cutter while riding the L train in Brooklyn to Harlem. No one comes to his aid in the subway car when he calls out. Vilma Kari, a sixty-five-year-old Filipina American is knocked to the ground and stomped in the face and stomach when going to church mid-afternoon near Times Square. Her pelvis is fractured. Two lobby workers in the nearby apartment building witnessing the attack do not intervene or call 911. None of these unprovoked assaults involve robberies; several involve racial slurs.

On March 16, 2021, in Atlanta, a twenty-one-year-old white man, Robert Aaron Long, targets massage businesses staffed and owned by Asian Americans, shooting and murdering six women of Asian descent, a white female customer, and a white handyman. He claims he's not a racist, blaming his sex addiction for the murders. After deliberating for an hour after getting a massage at one of the spas, he uses a gun purchased that day and kills Xiaojie Tan, forty-nine, a spa owner and mother who moved to the US fifteen years ago; Hyun Jung Grant, fifty-one, a single mom and schoolteacher from South Korea; Soon Chung Park, seventy-four, a cook and housekeeper who worked long days as a single mom to bring her five kids from Korea to the US; Suncha Kim, sixty-nine, a grandmother who cooked and cleaned while living at one of the spas; Yong Ae Yue, sixty-three, a South Korean mother of two; Delaina Ashley Yaun, thirty-three, a newlywed who had come for a couples massage with her husband; and Paul Andre Michels, fifty-four, who had been building a shelf at one of the spas.

At the press briefing after Long's interrogation, Captain Jay Baker of the Cherokee County Sheriff's Office states, "He was pretty much fed up and kind of at the end of his rope . . . Yesterday was a really bad day for him and this is what he did."[4] The year before, Baker posted a photo of a T-shirt printed with "Covid 19 imported virus from Chy-na" on Facebook, urging others to buy the same shirt.[5]

You wonder how many of the assailants involved in the 1,150 incidents of anti-Asian hate reported in Canada[6] and the 6,600 in the US[7] would say they were "fed up," "at the end of their rope," and "having a bad day." How many of them would believe it is perfectly permissible to use people of Asian descent as punching bags, targets for stabbing or shooting, handy scapegoats for accumulated frustration, despair, and rage. Openly. Publicly. As if there's no doubt that mainstream society is on their side, as if they represent mainstream public opinion. As if they believe their actions won't be sanctioned, but accepted. As if their victims won't or can't fight back—or don't even deserve to. And how about the "bad days" ahead for the children, siblings, partners, and extended family and friends of the murdered eight?

You ponder how the Cherokee County Sheriff's Office would have portrayed an Asian, Indigenous, Black, or Hispanic male mass murderer of six white women—as an animal, a monster, who had committed an inhuman, unjustifiable crime.

Will prosecutors and the public see through the perpetrator's blanket excuse of his "sex addiction" to investigate why Asian spas and massage parlors were targeted, and comb through the perpetrator's online porn browsing history? Will they acknowledge the long legacy of the western fetishization of Asian women embedded in popular culture from *Madama Butterfly* and *Miss Saigon* to *Full Metal Jacket*—subservient, compliant, self-sacrificing, sexually available, exotic? Will they understand what journalist Audrea Lim in the *New York Times* has noted,[8] that this fetishization is rooted in US military incursions in Asia, such as the sanctioned brothels in Japan servicing American troops in 1945, or the 300,000 sex workers in South Korea during and after the Korean War, many of whom worked in "camptowns" around

US military bases, or the thousands of sex workers in American bars during the Vietnam War? Or will this history of entitlement to commodify and exploit Asian women's bodies remain invisible because it is perceived as part of the natural order?

In the second year of the pandemic, you hope that anti-Asian racism is waning. Perhaps public outrage has found other outlets, other scapegoats. But just when you are about to become complacent, there's another assault. The police air the CCTV footage. A twenty-two-year-old Asian Canadian woman is walking east along West Georgia, a busy downtown street. You can't see her face in the video, just her dark coat, boots, dark hair. A white man is walking east. He's wearing yellow boots, a black jacket, a black shirt with a logo in the middle, a black toque and purple headphones, and carrying a blue bag. He suddenly lunges at the woman and tackles her. She is thrown against the wall of the hotel, behind a planter, and shoved down. She manages to escape and flee. It's 3:30 pm on a Friday afternoon, New Year's Eve on a busy sidewalk opposite the art gallery in front of a high-end hotel. How many other women has he attacked like this? A Japanese Canadian friend later tells you she thinks it's the man who assaulted her the year before—same yellow boots and purple headphones.

In her article "Spirit-Murdering the Messenger," law professor Patricia Williams argues we should see "racism as a crime, an offense so deeply painful and assaultive as to constitute something I call 'spirit-murder.' Society is only beginning to recognize that racism is as devastating, as costly, and as psychically obliterating as robbery or assault; indeed, they are often the same. Racism resembles other offenses against humanity whose structures are so deeply embedded in culture as to prove extremely resistant to being recognized as forms of oppression. It can be as difficult to prove as child abuse or rape, where the victim is forced to convince others that he or she was not at fault . . ."[9]

You expect that most of the 1,150 anti-Asian hate incidents reported in this country won't lead to prosecutions or convictions. There may not be witnesses or recorded evidence or sufficient information to identify a perpetrator or prove racist animus. Victims and witnesses might fear retaliation. They may face language barriers or mistrust the police. Or they may want to move on with their lives rather than wait over a year for a trial, reliving the crime. The dehumanizing and humiliating effects of hateful actions and words will still linger, undermining victims' fundamental sense of belonging.

The man who wrote "Drive them out of Canada," "Let's put a stop to ch**** coming to Canada" and "Shoot them on the spot" on the walls of Vancouver's Chinese Cultural Centre ends up pleading guilty to mischief against property, with the second charge of willfully promoting hatred being stayed. He reads an apology letter to the court blaming his actions on the media and insisting he is not racist. "I am not a hateful person. I don't hate Asian people. I was venting."[10]

Meanwhile, the cultural centre's windows are broken twenty-six times in one year. Graffiti continues to deface the walls of the cultural centre. Recently you read "Kill all your friends" on the walls of the cultural centre when you're heading to the Dr Sun Yat-Sen garden to hear a UBC professor give a presentation about historic Chinese Canadian communities throughout the province.

You wait as one month of the pandemic bleeds into the next. New variants emerge and take hold around the globe. The scapegoating and conspiracies continue, whether new, continuing, or revived, flourishing online across borders. Statistics gathered by the Institute for Strategic Dialogue indicate that violence motivated by right-wing extremism has increased 250 percent worldwide since before the pandemic, with new audiences being drawn into extremist right-wing ideology online, and right-wing extremists in Canada being influenced by violent right-wing extremism in the US. "The pandemic has . . . created a febrile environment for radicalization, by ensuring that millions of people have spent more time online. . . . [E]xtremist conspiracy theories have flourished and minority communities have been subject to increased hate crimes and harassment." In Canada, 2,467 right-wing extremist accounts generated forty-four million reactions in 2020, normalizing racist discourse that targets minorities.[11]

Members of the LGBTQ community are targeted. Muslim Canadian women wearing headscarves are targeted. There's the horrific murder of four members of a Muslim Pakistani-Canadian family by a young white supremacist driving a pickup truck. You can't control what will trigger another spate of irrational blaming and sudden violence. You keep hoping for the finger-pointing to stop. You keep hoping people might finally show signs of emerging from denial to finally unite and confront the climate crisis and the devastation of our ecosystems with conviction and urgency.

During the summer Olympics last August, you watch Maggie Mac Neil, an adoptee from China who was raised in London, Ontario, butterfly her way, half-fish, half-bird, to an Olympic gold medal in Tokyo. You wonder if her win might finally help move the tide toward acceptance over blame, just as the service of Chinese Canadian soldiers in World War II paved the way to the enfranchisement of Chinese Canadians and the end of the Chinese Exclusion Act. Will it take the grit, fierce finesse, courage, and superhuman devotion of an Olympic athlete or a squad of soldiers risking their lives to dismantle years of deeply entrenched distrust, suspicion, and prejudice each and every generation? Despite protest rallies and proposed legislation, perhaps true belonging will ultimately remain ephemeral or contingent, with any gains at risk of being erased by the next pandemic and looming civil, regional, and world wars. Meanwhile droughts continue, forests burn, towns are washed away, species after species disappear. No matter how you prepare, it seems more "bad days" are surely to come.

ENDNOTES

1   https://edmonton.citynews.ca/2020/07/14/charges-laid-following-racist-coronavirus-tirade/; https://www.narcity.com/edmonton/racist-edmonton-video-shows-a-man-aggressively-threatening-filipinocanadians-video

2   https://www.newyorker.com/news/daily-comment/the-atlanta-shooting-and-the-dehumanizing-of-asian-women

3   https://www.cbc.ca/news/canada/montreal/victim-hit-and-run-brossard-1.5756340

4   https://globalnews.ca/news/7704008/atlanta-spa-shootings-bad-day-racism/

5   https://www.forbes.com/sites/rachelsandler/2021/03/17/officer-who-said-atlanta-spa-shooter-was-having-a-bad-day-promoted-racist-covid-19-shirt-on-facebook/?sh=d6c3d0031edf

6   https://www.cbc.ca/news/canada/asian-racism-hate-canada-pandemic-1.5959788; https://globalnews.ca/news/7715260/anti-asian-racism-report-pandemic/://mcusercontent.com/9fbfd2cf7b2a8256f770fc35c/files/35c9daca-3fd4-46f4-a883c09b8c12bbca/covidracism_final_report.pdf; https://www.rcinet.ca/en/2021/03/24/new-report-finds-anti-asian-racist-incidents-on-the-rise-in-canada/

7   https://stopaapihate.org/national-report-through-march-2021/

8   https://www.nytimes.com/2018/01/06/opinion/sunday/alt-right-asian-fetish.html

9   https://repository.law.miami.edu/umlr/vol42/iss1/8/

10   https://bc.ctvnews.ca/240-day-sentence-for-man-behind-racist-graffiti-at-vancouver-chinese-cultural-centre-1.5723771; https://www.vancouverisawesome.com/local-news/despicable-man-who-wrote-hateful-graffiti-on-vancouvers-chinese-cultural-centre-sentenced-4908031

11   https://www.cbc.ca/news/canada/british-columbia/racists-attacks-court-hate-crimes-1.5604912

Kyo Maclear

GIVERNY

In her early fifties, after her husband left and when she felt at the edge of the earth, about to fall off, my mother travelled to Giverny. She wanted to see the inspiration for Claude Monet's *Nymphéas*. To say that these were challenging days for my mother would be an understatement. A marriage is a counterweight, and while she had never been compliantly or happily married, it was frightening to her, unimaginable, to suddenly spring forth into the world. This was not the future she had expected for herself or the tale she had inhabited for decades. She decided, impulsively, to use some of her savings to go to Giverny at the very moment she was being asked to forge a completely new life, to assume another form.

*

Monet's work became an obsession; his loose, almost abstract paintings of lily pads grabbed hold of her. I have spent most of my life wondering why people love what and whom they do, why we fasten onto certain others. To me, Monet's paintings had always seemed too pretty, exuding an air of powdery sweetness that reminded me of Yardley soap. As a child, toted along on museum pilgrimages, I preferred the heavy lines and geometrical shapes of Joan Miró and Paul Klee. I didn't understand my mother's washy tastes, her appetite for dissolving and sparkling landscapes. All that echoing light. There was no centre to these swirling and frothing paintings! Anytime I tried to find a place to focus, my eyes were drawn everywhere around. But maybe that was the point and a clue to the effect they had on her. Here was art you could disappear inside. Here was a place to lose yourself, a place to gaze rather than be gazed upon. Of course, I am speculating. No one teaches you to see through your mother's eyes.

*

For my mother, it wasn't just Monet. She loved J. M. W. Turner for his watercolour sketches of the sea. Shikō Munakata for his trees. Joan Mitchell for her sunflowers. What entranced her were paintings that tossed the viewer into a big absorbing picture space where the world became less solid, more atmospheric. The artists she most admired seemed to share a common under-standing: it isn't always easy to set down what you see or say what you mean. I found it almost unbearable as a child not to know what I was looking at, but if I said so, she would simply reply: *It's paint.*

*

Monet moved to Giverny, forty-five miles outside of Paris, in 1883, at the exact midpoint of his life. He had been looking for a place that combined water, field, and light. He immediately set about gardening, planting weeping willows by the water and, of course, water lilies in the pond. He arrayed the garden with pink roses, red geraniums, deep-purple pansies, impatiens, lavender, and peonies. In an area where people cultivated land for food and not for apparent pleasure, Monet's horticultural choices were regarded with suspicion.

*

When my mother arrived at Giverny, it was a late-August afternoon; clouds were moving in. Her small tour group was rushed directly inside to see the water lilies before the garden closed for the day. My mother took a slow walk by the lily pond. In the summer sun, the pond was a simple reflective blue. Then the sky darkened—a cloud passed in front of the sun—and the pond and the lilies trembled and changed.

*

Monet's eyesight began to fail not long after he moved to Giverny. Cloudy with cataracts, his eyes would approach blindness in his later years. By 1922, when he looked at the pond, he would describe it as seeing "through a fog." It became "more vast and chartless the closer [Monet's] gaze approached," writes the art historian Kirk Varnedoe.

*

My mother stood in the spitting rain, the prickled pond now the purple-grey of irises. She was prepared to stay by her marriage, just as Monet had stood by that pond, growing a wild white beard to his knees, returning to the same subject over and over. She was prepared to stay in that tempestuous, tender, painful, destabilizing relationship, a union built on loyalty that defied reason, until the end of her days. Then it disintegrated, and the world became less solid, more wavering.

*

The lily pond was not the only repeated motif in Monet's work. As an undergraduate art history student, I studied the twenty paintings he did of Rouen Cathedral in the 1890s, absorbed the flickering movement of light and shifting weather conditions, a way of seeing that would eventually lead to his famous *Nymphéas*. I can still hear the sound of the slide carousel advancing as my professor droned on about optical elements. I felt a sort of happy metaphysical vertigo, as the fan whirred and pictures flashed in the dark room, understanding the paintings as a lesson in inexhaustibility, a lesson in the churning and changing world—a lesson that feels less terrifying and more exhilarating when you are eighteen and, frankly, less exhausted by the idea of limitlessness.

*

Many years later, I would read John Berger describe these paintings as "systematic proof that the history of painting would never be the same again. This history had henceforward to admit that every appearance could be thought of as a mutation and that visibility itself should be considered flux." There was no right way to gaze upon the world, in other words. No ideal set of conditions.

*

My mother stood by the pond as the rain fell faster—soft speedy droplets. She stood where the artist had painted his famous *Nymphéas*, paintings that tried and tried again, capturing the nature of light vaporizing form and narrative. Monet worked on the water lilies as World War I flared around him, as the sound of artillery erupted in the distance and his son and stepson were sent to the front to fight for France.

*

Monet's paintings, which conveyed a painter's decomposing reality, were derided by some, including Paul Cézanne, for their insufficient and formless sense of structure. For other critics, the structure was there even if it was not painted or expressed directly. It was present in the mood of softness bordered by solidity, in a view of a world edged by turbulence, in brush strokes that registered perceptual upheaval, a canvas recording forces and feelings beyond pure light and weather. A man turns inward while feeling the storm at his back.

*

My mother walked around Giverny. This was how she chose to mark her independence.

*

To what do we commit ourselves and for how long? Monet painted the *Nymphéas* 247 times. "It took me some time to understand my water lilies," he wrote. The older I get, the more I understand this impulse toward reduction and repetition; the more I understand there is infinitude in a spartan focus, in Agnes Martin's geometries, in Giorgio Morandi's vases. Focalizing can be regenerative even for those of us who believe the sprawling clamour of the world demands our promiscuous attention.

*

Two hundred and forty-seven times. A marriage may have as many incarnations, some more satisfying, some more frustrating than others. Love can be revised and resurrected after a long dormancy. It is possible, when a couple finally collapses, to grieve the better incarnations that are also dissolved.

*

There is a photograph of Derek Jarman by the pond at Giverny, standing on the small arched Japanese bridge against a blooming bank of wisteria. Jarman visited many famous gardens, but this was to be his final excursion before his death from AIDS complications in 1994. Like Monet's, his sight was failing, and perhaps this deepened the bond he felt with the earlier artist. In *Smiling in Slow Motion*, Jarman describes Giverny as a "delight" and "the shaggiest garden in the world," surely a compliment for a place tended by ten full-time gardeners and coming from an artist-plantsman who celebrated shagginess as coup against the monotony of too much human agency. ("If a garden isn't shaggy, forget it.")

*

Giverny is a garden that verges, in areas, on Orientalist kitsch. Jarman was called there just as my mother was called there, as if summoned by a courtesy phone. They had no adjoining or mutual story, but they shared an eagerness to stand by a lily pond. Perhaps Giverny is where you go when you need a measure of hope or are trying to make a transformation endurable. Maybe it is a place to mark death—whether the demise of a marriage, the passing of a life stage, or a more literal ending. Joan Mitchell was "trying to get out of a violent phase and into something else," she said in 1964, a few years before moving to Vétheuil, just up the hill from Monet's house.

⁕

The visitors were told they had twenty more minutes. The rain was now a light drizzle, the pond cloaked in wet, floating mist. My mother chose to spend her last moment by the bamboo grove, which she felt was all the more special because it was an area of the garden Monet never painted. Then she shook drops from her sleeves, went to the gift shop, and bought a single blue-and-yellow dinner plate and a fridge magnet. When she returned from Giverny, after she had stood on the Japanese bridge, looking upon the wisteria and water lilies, she allowed her life to become abundant and untamed. The shagginess of Monet's garden was so different from the paintings. Time had made it so.

⁕

Monet once said, "For me, it is only the surrounding atmosphere which gives subjects their true value." I would like to be a writer who, if I cannot convey things in themselves, captures the air as it touches the world. If I cannot tell my mother's story, I want to tell her atmosphere.

Sandy Pool

///////

I LOVE LUCY

"I am a reflection of my mother's secret poetry
as well as her hidden angers"
—Audre Lorde

"I don't know how to tell a joke. I never tell jokes. I can tell
stories that happened to me . . . anecdotes. But never a joke."
—Lucille Ball

JOB SWITCHING

In this scene, my mother stands facing an assembly line. She is
wearing a chef's hat so big it looks like a soufflé collapsed on her
head. I am standing beside her, and in between us towers a pin-
straight woman, my mother's mother. "All right girls," my
mother's mother says in a heavy Dutch accent, "now this is your
last chance. If one piece of candy gets past you and into the packing room unwrapped, YOU'RE FIRED." "Yes ma'am," My mother
says, and I nod enthusiastically. "LET ER ROOLLLLLL" my

mother's mother belts into another room. The assembly line doesn't start, and my mother's mother looks around, furious and embarrassed. She tries again in a more militaristic tone: "LET ER ROLLLLLLLL" and the whole apparatus starts to move. My mother's mother leaves the room.

I look to my mother so I know what to do. At first, the conveyer belt moves very slowly, and we both manage to wrap our chocolates. My mother is wrapping her chocolates and leaving every other chocolate, so I have something to wrap too. Soon, though, the conveyor speeds up.

My mother panics immediately. I watch as my mother starts shoving chocolates in her mouth as if to hide them. She knows she is out of her depth, but there is nothing she can do now.

It is embarrassing to watch my mother struggle this way and even more embarrassing that I am struggling with her. I put two chocolates in my mouth and gag on them. Soon, both of us are shoving chocolate wherever we can: down our bras, into our soufflé hats. We cannot let my mother's mother see us in this state. "Listen," my mother says. "I think we're fighting a losing game."

We are stuffed with sweets to twice our size when suddenly the conveyor belt irks to a stop and my mother's mother marches back in. My mother flashes a panicked chipmunk smile.

"Ahhhh," my mother's mother says, "you are doing splendidly. Speed it up, Al!"

LUCY HAS HER EYES EXAMINED

Here comes the joke: My mother's mother calls the shots, and my mother scrambles to please her. My mother's mother barks orders, and my mother salutes. My mother's mother makes royal proclamations, and my mother holds the scroll. Everyone loves my mother's mother. Everyone fears my mother's mother. My mother's mother is very witty. My mother's mother barks at my mother. My mother panics. My mother barks at me. I panic. Everyone loves my mother. My mother is very witty. The laugh track rolls maniacally.

LUCY TELLS THE TRUTH

The truth is that my mother did not have a nice mother. It was a family show, but it was not a comedy. My mother's mother shoved my mother into scratchy dresses. My mother's mother said judgmental and unkind things. My mother's mother told my mother, "You are not very smart." My mother's mother told my mother, "I am going to pinch you, but only in places where bruises won't show."

My mother's mother berated my mother in front of her father, in front of her brothers, in front of her neighbours, in front of her children. When I was sixteen, my mother's mother suddenly proclaimed my high school boyfriend was a piece of garbage. When I told my mother what happened, my mother called her mother and demanded an apology. We lived ten minutes away, but my mother's mother didn't speak to us for five years.

We used to see my mother's mother downtown. My mother's mother glared at us in lines at the post office. My mother's mother glared at us in lines at the drug store. My mother's mother glared at us in lines at the Valu-mart. I could not understand how a such a small thing could undo our entire family. To everyone except my family, my mother's mother was still as funny and charming as Lucille Ball.

My mother's father died calling out for my mother, but my mother's mother did not call my mother to let her know. When we showed up for the funeral, my mother's mother did not act as if she hadn't spoken to us for five years. She acted like she was all caught up.

This was not easy for my mother. She went to therapy. She did therapeutic exercises. One day she threw a dozen eggs at a blown-up picture of my mother's mother she set up in the backyard.

By the time I was sixteen, my mother had also become sick. She took a lot of pills, many of which I could not pronounce. One night she drank a lot, too, and ended up naked and screaming at us from inside a closet. Then she took the car over to the parking lot of the hockey arena, and we all took turns getting in the car with her, where she said, "You are a horrible, awful slut and I hope you fry." "You are an ungrateful little cretin and I stood up for you and look where it got me. Nowhere. Totally nothing." The next day, she remembered none of the things she said. There were no apologies. My father was there, too, but he never thought to stop her.

My mother tried her best. And I tried my best. Probably my mother's mother tried her best too. My mother's best was never good enough for my mother's mother, and my best was never good enough either. It was not a very good show, or a very interesting show. The jokes were stale by then, but they were comforting.

THE CHARM SCHOOL

The punchline was that my mother was a covert narcissist but didn't know it. The punchline involved both intentional violence and violence by mishaps, often resulting from the inept use of props. The punchline was that my mother was my friend. The punchline was that my mother was my enemy. The punchline was that I was a reflection of my mother. The punchline was still very funny. The real punchline was that my mother was a Punch and Judy bully. Her sight gags were impeccable—the double take, the collide, the fall, the feint, the roar. Her silent jabs could sink ships, superglue lips. She could cook a roast and roast you at the same time—sirloin, tenderloin, T-bone, rump, pot roast, chuck roast, oxtail, stump. The real punchline was something about vaudeville, but my mother was not a funnyman or a buffoon. The real punchline was that her narcissistic injury came from her mother, but I didn't know it. The magic show was only for family. There was no one to warn me about the punchline that was coming.

My mother was a master of uninhibited action. All smoke, all mirrors. She could make you doubt the colour of blouse you were wearing. She could make you feel like a piece of garbage. She could make you feel like the most selfish person in the world. The real punchline was that the routine was not only pre-set but started before I was born. Everyone still laughed at my mother's punchlines. They were afraid not to.

LUCY DOES THE TANGO

In this scene, my mother and I are stuffing our shirts and bras full of eggs. This is not the start of the scene. The premise of the scene is that my mother and I have been trying to raise hens for eggs together, but our hens won't lay eggs. My mother and I decide to buy eggs from the store, and now we are stuffing the eggs down our shirts to take them outside and deposit the store-bought eggs under the hens. We don't want my father to find out the plan we hatched has already failed. As usual, our scheme is over-complicated, but neither of us has any better ideas.

My mother and I are just about to head out when Ricky unexpectedly appears at the top of the stairs. Ricky has very bad timing or perfect timing. Ricky says he booked himself on a later train because he wants to rehearse a tango number with my mother. Ricky says "Now come on. I haven't got much time. It's either now or never." My mother shoots me a look. "Let's make it never?" As a person, my mother wants to avoid playing this gag, but as an actor she knows better. As an actor, my mother knows the gag only works when drawn out to its completely inevitable conclusion. I try to leave the scene, but Ricky says, "Now, Ethel, wait a minute. Stick around. I want ya to see what, you know, tell us what it looks like." I want to tell Ricky to stop the scene. I want to tell Ricky I already know the ending. My mother tries to get away, too, but Ricky won't let her go. "Come on" Ricky says "I wanna do the finish." "The finish?" My mother asks, as if she doesn't know what that looks like. Ricky spins my egg-swollen mother out with a tight flick of the wrist. My mother flinches preemptively.

We all know the finish. The finish is about failure—that old bedraggled number. The finish is about the failure we know is coming and how funny that failure is when it arrives. The finish requires my mother to stand in a puddle of her failure like a thousand broken eggs for a full sixty-five seconds, while the studio audience laughs. The finish is me, with a shirt full of unbroken unfertilized eggs, watching my mother, waiting for my turn. The finish is timing. The finish is Ricky, the enabler, after a

long pause, saying, "Now, Lucy, I know this is a ridiculous question, but what are you doing with eggs under your shirt?" and
Lucy, with a straight face, answering, "Trying to hatch them?"

LUCY AND THE DUMMY

The truth is that Lucy did not have an easy childhood, and I did
not have an easy childhood. Our mothers were not capable of the
kind of love we wanted. Our mothers could not meet our needs.
We could not see these patterns clearly, but we felt them. In this
way, our on-screen chemistry is undeniable. We work together like
stunt doubles, or best friends. When my mother flinches, I flinch.

LUCY GETS INTO PICTURES

Scene: I am seven years old. My sister and I tiptoe around the
house because my mother is sleeping. We are all afraid to wake
her in case she wakes up furious about the laundry or the dishes
or the weather. Instead, we watch ten episodes of *I Love Lucy* on
VHS tapes, because we are also afraid to change the channel.

Scene: I am eleven years old. I am sobbing in the bathroom and
blood is dripping down my legs. I wad up toilet paper and shove
it in my underwear, hoping it will stop. Later, my mother finds a
bloody pair of underwear in the laundry. She slaps me across the
face and sends me upstairs to learn how to use a tampon, alone.

Scene: I have been scratching myself and have developed a
disordered relationship with food. My mother comes in and sees
the scratches. She asks what people will think of her if they see
me like this. She slaps me so hard I hit my head on the floor. We
never discuss it again.

Scene: I am twenty, and my mother is angry. She accuses my boyfriend of kicking her dog. My boyfriend did not kick her dog, and I try to explain the dog was humping his leg. My mother is not angry at my boyfriend. My mother is angry at me for not calling home enough. My mother says if we don't apologize for kicking her dog, we are no longer welcome in her home. My mother does not speak to me for a year. When I return home, my mother acts as if she is all caught up. Lucy has no 'splainin' to do.

Scene: I am thirty-eight years old sitting beside her in the hospice. "You know," my mother says, "I never understood you." "Oh yeah?" I say. "Do you feel like you gave birth to an alien?" "Not when you were little," she says. "You really were so very very sweet."

LUCY RAISES TULIPS

It can be hard to love a narcissistic mother. But my mother and I love our narcissistic mothers more than anything. We bring our mothers roses. We bring our mothers tulips. What else is there to do? Our mothers are the centre of our universe. And what is a solar system without a sun? Our narcissistic mothers need us, and we need them. When we finally stand up to our narcissistic mothers, we are slapped so hard we see entire constellations. We won't do that again.

LUCY AND HARPO MARX

In this scene, Lucy is dressed like Harpo Marx, and I am also dressed like Harpo Marx. Our goal is to reproduce the mirror scene from *Duck Soup*, which was originally performed in 1933.

We have been rehearsing this scene for years, but I am still nervous. I am supposed to hide behind a door and then pop out wearing my crumpled top hat and curly orange wig. As an actor, I know the goal is to play this scene perfectly—to be an exact mirror for Lucy, who is also wearing a top hat and a curly orange wig.

When we step out from either side of the door, the resemblance is uncanny: the same goofy expressions, the same sidelong glances. When Lucy raises her arms, my arms move as if guided by an unseen force. My legs kick out with the grace of a synchronized swimmer. Like any method actor, I attempt to differentiate the art of experiencing with the art of representation, but it is difficult to know exactly where the edges are.

I dive back behind the door. This, too, is scripted. In the distance, I can hear the audience laughing, and I imagine my mother on the other side, hamming it up for the cameras; poking out her bottom lip, widening her eyes, and lifting her arms in a gesture of fake confusion.

When we step out again, my mother is suddenly less focused. She moves less deliberately and begins lifting her limbs in unpredictable ways. I try to keep up, but her gestures are manic. We call cut several times. I am so rattled that I honk my horn with the wrong hand. I begin to worry about Lucy as a person, but it is too late. Lucy has already decided what kind of scene this will be.

The truth is I cannot be Lucy and Lucy cannot be Lucy either. Lucy cannot be my real mother Lucy Pool or my fake mother Lucille Ball or my fake mother Lucy Ricardo. I cannot be the fake Ethel Mertz or the fake Vivian Vance or the real Vivian Roberta Jones or the real me, Sandy Pool. This essay is not about my fake mother Lucille Ball or my fake mother Lucy Ricardo. This essay is about slapstick, and the sight gags we use to mediate the pain of not being able to be ourselves.

LUCY IS ENVIOUS

Online, I find a cocktail recipe for narcissistic mothers. The internet recommends mixing 1 oz guilt, 1 oz shame, 1 oz blame and 1 oz envy. The internet quips we should garnish with rage, then splash the drink in our own faces. But narcissistic mothers are no joke. When my mother dies, I find no jokes in her notebook. I find only a single poem scrawled on a nuclear orange scrap of paper: "I've reached the October of my life / the leaves scattered out /across the ground." I did not want my mother to be a poet. I wanted her to be a self that was also at my service. I did not want her orange sickness, her orange suffering, her orange vulnerability. I did not want to feel responsible for bringing on the deadness in her.

When *I Love Lucy* was cancelled, Lucille Ball also tried acting in a variety of spin-offs; *The Lucy Show*, *Here's Lucy*, *Life With Lucy*. Lucy was all the public ever wanted from Lucille Ball. And then one day, they wouldn't buy her as Lucy either. That was the real tragedy of her life.

The truth of my life is that I loved my mother, Lucy Pool. I never wanted my mother to die simply so I could live.

LUCY HATES TO LEAVE

Any decent vaudevillian will tell you the mirror bit is built on impossibility. Even the best mirror bits are a second or two out of sync. My mother could not be the real Lucy Pool or my fake mother Lucy Ricardo because she was too busy trying to be the perfect mirror. For a while the illusion was convincing, but not forever.

When my mother's mirror bit flopped, my mother's mother was furious. She gaslit, she guilt-tripped, she played victim, she flipped the script. My mother's performance was never good enough for my mother's mother. My mother did not know failure was built into the performance, and started before she was born. The truth is I wanted to please my mother, but the mirror bit is built on impossibility. Even the best mirror bits are a second or two out of sync. I could not be the real Sandy Pool because I was too busy trying to be the perfect mirror.

For a while the illusion was convincing, but not forever. When my mirror bit flopped, my mother was furious. She gaslit, she guilt-tripped, she played victim, she flipped the script. My performance was never good enough, but it was still comforting.

When my mother died, my therapist said I would feel grief, and I do.

She said I would feel relief, and I do. This does not mean I did not love my mother.

LUCY AND THE LOVING CUP

After my mother died, my sister said my mother wanted to give me a cup. The cup was in a box somewhere in the basement. My mother had looked for hours and hours, but she could not find the cup. I had bought her the cup in 1994 from a garage sale. The cup said "Welcome To 40. It's all downhill from here!" The cup had a picture of a man sliding down a bumpy mountain. My mother kept the cup for twenty-six years to give me on my fortieth birthday. But she died when I was thirty-eight. When I think of the cup, I feel like crying. It was her idea of a joke, of course, but by then the punchline was missing.

LUCY'S SHOWBIZ SWAN SONG

Through the magic of film, I stand facing my mother again. In this scene, my mother is dressed to the nines, in a powder blue organza swing dress and her trademark swoop of ebony hair.

Under the studio lights, her eyes shine dark and wet. She extends her arm to me in a dramatic sweep that only looks natural on television—my cue.

My mother's legato fills the studio and I instinctively start to sway: "That's life (that's life) I tell ya, I can't deny it. I thought of quitting, baby, but my heart ain't gonna buy it . . ."

Lucy swings me around the room, my blue eyes blinking back at her. She leads with the grace of a woman who is both a winner and a struggler—a consummate performer who knows that to laugh is to identify and to identify is to know the boundaries of our bodies. We dance for hours before the outro: "But if there's nothing shaking come this here July . . ."

Lucy knows what the audience wants is a story with a beginning, a middle, and a finish. My mother turns me out with a quick flick of the wrist.

"I'm gonna roll myself up in a big ball . . ."

For once, we do the finish. The finish is flawless.

The finish is heaven, you see, because I finally love Lucy, yes, I love Lucy and Lucy loves me.

CONTRIBUTORS' BIOGRAPHIES

LYNDSIE BOURGON is a writer, oral historian, and National Geographic Explorer based in British Columbia. She writes about the environment and its entanglement with history, culture, and identity, and her features have been published in the *Atlantic, Smithsonian*, the *Guardian*, the *Oxford American, Aeon, The Walrus*, and *Hazlitt*, among other outlets. Her first book, *Tree Thieves: Crime and Survival in North America's Woods*, was longlisted for the 2023 PEN/John Kenneth Galbraith Award for Nonfiction and was a finalist for the Columbia School of Journalism J. Anthony Lukas Book Award.

NICOLE BOYCE's work has appeared in *The Awl, CV2, Event, The Fiddlehead, Grain, Joyland, McSweeney's Internet Tendency, Prairie Fire, Riddle Fence*, and more. She was the winner of the 2016 *Prairie Fire* Nonfiction Contest and placed third in EVENT's 2021 Nonfiction Contest. Her writing has also been shortlisted for *The New Quarterly*'s Peter Hinchcliffe Fiction Award and longlisted for CBC's Nonfiction Prize. She received her MFA from UBC's Creative Writing Program, where she was the Prose Editor of *PRISM international*.

ROBERT COLMAN is a Newmarket, Ontario–based writer and editor. His fourth collection of poems, *Ghost Work*, will be published with Palimpsest Press in 2024.

DANIEL ALLEN COX is the author of *I Felt the End Before It Came: Memoirs of a Queer Ex-Jehovah's Witness*, and four novels nominated for the Lambda Literary, Ferro-Grumley, and ReLit Awards. His novel *Mouthquake* was one of twenty-seven works selected for inclusion in *QuébeQueer*, a fifty-year overview of queer cultural production in Quebec. Daniel's essays and short fiction have appeared in *Electric Literature*, *Literary Hub*, *The Malahat Review*, *The Florida Review*, *Maisonneuve*, *Catapult*, *TriQuarterly*, *The Rumpus*, *The Advocate*, *Best Gay Stories*, *Fourth Genre: Explorations in Nonfiction*, and elsewhere. His essay "The Glow of Electrum" was nominated for a 2021 National Magazine Award and was named a notable essay in *The Best American Essays 2021*. Daniel is past president of the Quebec Writers' Federation and is final judge for *The Malahat Review*'s 2023 Constance Rooke Creative Nonfiction Prize.

ACADIA CURRAH (she/they) is an essayist and playwright residing in Vancouver, currently attending the University of British Columbia. She is a leather-jacket-wearing, latte-toting lesbian; her work seeks to reach those who most need to hear it.

Their work has appeared in *The Spotlong Review*, *Defunkt Magazine*, *Other Worldly Women Press*, the *South Florida Poetry Journal*, and *The Fiddlehead*.

SADIQA DE MEIJER is a writer of Dutch-Kenyan-Pakistani-Afghani origins and has lived in Canada since the age of twelve. Her writing often has to do with landscape, language, motherhood, medicine, spirituality, and migration. Her poems have won the CBC Poetry Prize, *Arc*'s Poem of the Year Competition, and other honours, and been published in *Poetry* and *Brick* magazines. Her two poetry collections are *Leaving Howe Island* (Oolichan Books, 2013), which was a finalist for the Governor General's Literary Award, and *The Outer Wards* (Véhicule Press, 2020), a finalist for the Raymond Souster Award. Her essays have been short-listed for *The New Quarterly*'s Edna Staebler Personal Essay Contest and *The Malahat Review*'s Constance Rooke Nonfiction Prize, and been published in Canada, the UK, and the US. Her third book, *alfabet/alphabet: a memoir of a first language* (Palimpsest Press, 2020), won the Governor General's Literary Award. She is currently working on new collections of poetry and essays.

GABRIELLE DROLET is a writer and cartoonist based in Montreal. Her work, which focuses on culture and accessibility, has appeared in *The Walrus*, the *Globe and Mail*, the *New Yorker*, the *New York Times*, and more. She graduated with an MFA in creative writing from the University of Guelph in 2023. She really, really loves pre-minced garlic.

Dr HAMED ESMAEILION was born in Kermanshah, Iran. He grew up in a middle-class family during the Iran-Iraq war that ravaged the western part of Iran, including his hometown. While in Iran, Esmaeilion published four novels that earned awards from the top Iranian literary circles. His first novel, *Thyme is not Pretty*, won the Hooshang Golshiri Award for best short story collection, and his third book, *Dr Datis*, won the Hooshang Golshiri Award for best novel. *Gamasiab Has No Fish* was critically acclaimed and subsequently banned by the Islamic Republic authorities. Hamed published his next novel, *The Blue Toukan*, in the United Kingdom.

Esmaeilion lost his wife and daughter who were aboard Ukrainian flight PS752 that was shot down by IRGC missiles over Tehran on January 8, 2020. He published his memories in the aftermath of the tragedy in *It Snows In This House*. During the lead-up to the downing of flight PS752, Esmaeilion was working on two novels, *The Fractured Diaries of the Chancellor* and *The Summer with Five Bullets*. He published the last three books under Pareera Publishing, which he founded in honour of his wife and daughter.

Since losing his wife and daughter, Esmaeilion has dedicated his life to revealing the truth behind the heinous crime of the downing of flight PS752 and bringing the perpetrators to justice. He was a leading figure in the formation of the Association of Families of Flight PS752 Victims in Canada. His efforts on behalf of the Association have been instrumental in affecting the discourse in the legal and governmental activities relating to the case.

KATE GIES teaches creative nonfiction and expressive arts in a trauma-informed program at George Brown College in Toronto. Her writing has appeared in *The Malahat Review, Hobart, The*

Humber Literary Review, the *Minola Review*, and other places. Her memoir about her childhood medical experiences related to a missing ear is forthcoming from Simon & Schuster Canada. More of her work can be found at kategies.com.

A settler writer, educator, and critic from Kjipuktuk (Halifax), DAVID HUEBERT (he/him) teaches literature and creative writing at the University of New Brunswick. His fiction has won the CBC Short Story Prize and was a finalist for the 2020 Journey Prize. David's fiction debut, *Peninsula Sinking*, won a Dartmouth Book Award and was runner-up for the Danuta Gleed Literary Award. His latest book, *Chemical Valley* (Biblioasis, 2021), won the Alistair MacLeod Prize for Short Fiction and was shortlisted for the Thomas Raddall Atlantic Fiction Award. David's debut novel, *Oil People*, will be published by McClelland & Stewart in 2024.

JENNY HWANG is a Korean-Canadian writer and mother. Her writing explores her diasporic experience and the legacies of colonialism, war, and immigration passed down through generations. Her "Silkworms" essay won *The Fiddlehead*'s 2022 Creative Nonfiction Contest. She is enrolled in the MFA in Creative Writing program at the University of Guelph and has previously worked as an immigration lawyer and in refugee resettlement with Canada's Private Sponsorship of Refugees program. She lives with her partner and three children in Mississauga, Ontario.

FIONA TINWEI LAM has authored three poetry collections, *Intimate Distances* (Nightwood Editions, 2002), *Enter the*

Chrysanthemum (Caitlin Press, 2009), and *Odes & Laments* (Caitlin Press, 2019) and a children's book, *The Rainbow Rocket* (Oolichan Books, 2014). Her poems have been included in *Best Canadian Poetry* (2010, 2017 anniversary edition, and 2020) and thrice with BC's Poetry in Transit program, as well as featured in several award-winning poetry videos made in collaboration with filmmakers and animators that have screened at festivals internationally. She edited *The Bright Well: Contemporary Canadian Poems about Facing Cancer* (Leaf Press, 2011), and co-edited two nonfiction anthologies, *Double Lives: Writing and Motherhood* (McGill-Queen's University Press, 2008) with Cathy Stonehouse and Shannon Cowan, and *Love Me True: Writers Reflect on the Ins, Outs, Ups & Downs of Marriage* (Caitlin Press, 2018) with Jane Silcott. Shortlisted for the City of Vancouver Book Prize and other awards, her work appears in over 45 anthologies, including *Slice Me Some Truth: An Anthology of Canadian Nonfiction* (Wolsak & Wynn 2011). Her nonfiction has also appeared in *Maisonneuve*, the *Globe and Mail*, *The Tyee*, *The Fiddlehead*, EVENT, and *The New Quarterly*. A former lawyer, she teaches creative writing at Simon Fraser University Continuing Studies and is Vancouver's sixth poet laureate. fionalam.net.

KYO MACLEAR is an essayist, novelist, editor, and children's author. Her books have been translated into eighteen languages, published in over twenty-five countries, and garnered nominations from the Hilary Weston Writers' Trust Prize for Nonfiction, the Governor General's Literary Awards, the TD Canadian Children's Literature Awards, the Boston Globe–Horn Book Awards, the Amazon.ca First Novel Award, and the National Magazine Awards. Her nonfiction books include the hybrid memoir *Birds*

Art Life (2017), winner of the Trillium Book Award, and *Unearthing* (Knopf and Scribner, 2023). She teaches creative writing with the University of Guelph Creative Writing MFA. kyomaclear.com, kyomaclearkids.com.

SANDY POOL (she/they) is a Canadian essayist, poet, and Professor of Creative Writing. Her first collection of poetry, *Exploding into Night* was nominated for the Governor General's Award for Poetry. Her second collection, *Undark: An Oratorio*, was nominated for Ontario's Trillium Book Award for Poetry, an Alberta Book Award, and a Toronto Arts Award. Her third book, *If Body/Freedom*, a book of nonfiction essays has been awarded a variety of prestigious fellowships, including residencies at Yaddo, Berton House, the Siena Art Institute, and the Dora Maar House. She has taught English and Creative Writing at a variety of post-secondary institutions in Canada, the United States, and the United Kingdom, including teaching in the MFA program at the UK's most prestigious program in Creative Writing, the University of East Anglia. Currently, she is an Associate Professor in Creative Writing and Literature and divides her time between Canada and New York.

PUBLICATIONS CONSULTED FOR THE 2024 EDITION

Aeon, Antigonish Review, Arc Poetry Magazine, BC Bookworld, Border Crossings, Brick, Canada's History, Canadian Literature, Canadian Notes & Queries, Dalhousie Review, [EDIT], EVENT, Exile Quarterly, The Fiddlehead, filling Station, Geist, Globe and Mail, Grain, Granta, Hazlitt, Herizons, Literary Review of Canada, Maisonneuve, The Malahat Review, Minola Review, The Nashwaak Review, The New Quarterly, New York Times, Newfoundland Quarterly, Open Minds Quarterly, Parentheses Journal, Prairie Fire, PRISM international, Queen's Quarterly, Quillette, Room, Spacing, The /temz/ Review, Toronto Life, The Tyee, University of Toronto Quarterly, The Walrus

ACKNOWLEDGEMENTS

"Ruffled Feathers: How Feral Peacocks Divided a Small Town" by Lyndsie Bourgon first appeared in *The Walrus*. Reprinted by permission of the author.

"One Route, Over and Over" by Nicole Boyce first appeared in EVENT. Reprinted by permission of the author.

"Every Saturday" by Robert Colman first appeared in *Canadian Notes & Queries*. Reprinted by permission of the author.

"You Can't Blame Movers for Everything Broken" by Daniel Allen Cox first appeared in *The Malahat Review*. Reprinted by permission of the author.

"Femme Fatales and the Lavender Menace" by Acadia Currah first appeared in *The Fiddlehead*. Reprinted by permission of the author.

"Do No Harm" by Sadiqa de Meijer first appeared in *Geist*. Reprinted by permission of the author.

EDITOR'S BIOGRAPHY

MARCELLO DI CINTIO is the author of four books, including *Walls: Travels Along the Barricades,* which won the Shaughnessy Cohen Prize for Political Writing and the W. O. Mitchell City of Calgary Book Prize, and *Pay No Heed to the Rockets: Palestine in the Present Tense*—also a W. O. Mitchell Prize winner. Di Cintio's magazine writing has appeared in publications such as *The International New York Times, The Walrus, Canadian Geographic* and *Afar*. Di Cintio has served as a writer-in-residence at the Calgary Public Library, the University of Calgary, and the Palestine Writing Workshop, and he teaches nonfiction writing at the annual WordsWorth youth writing residency.